Marriage Made *easier*

Advance Praise

"This is such a powerful and important book! So many people stay in unhappy, unhealthy or unfulfilling partnerships because of fear, confusion or just plain habit. Kathryn MacIntyre provides you with wonderful step-by-step processes to move you toward greater happiness and emotional freedom. She shows you how to evaluate your circumstances, gain a deeper clarity, asses your real feelings, discover real and tangible solutions, and find the courage to take action. Focusing on the problem keeps you stuck; focusing on the solution moves you forward. This book offers real solutions to move you forward!"

Pamala Oslie, Author of *Life Colors,*
Make Your Dreams Come True, and *Infinite You*

"This is a great book for anyone considering divorce. Whether you are looking for help to keep the marriage together or are lacking the courage to go forward with the final step, this book helps you get clear on what you really want by asking questions about yourself and where your emotions are coming from. Together with the many techniques, exercises and meditations throughout the book you can find clarity on issues that you may be carrying and weren't even aware of. This books helps you get to the root cause of why you are considering divorce and how to navigate your way through or help you save your marriage."

Deborah Hanks, Barnes & Noble

"I wish I would have had this book at the start of my divorce. It would have saved me a lot of stress, fear and heartache. Kathryn gives you the tools you need to get through a very challenging time with your dignity and integrity intact. Divorce doesn't have to be a catastrophe. You can go through it consciously and come out happier and healthier on the other side. Kathryn is that trusted friend to guide you through it with compassion and love!"

Jenny Lockhart, Relish Life Coaching

Marriage
Made
easier

7 Steps
to Making
Life Better

Kathryn MacIntyre

NEW YORK

LONDON • NASHVILLE • MELBOURNE • VANCOUVER

Marriage Made *easier*
7 Steps to Making Life Better

Published in New York, New York, by Morgan James Publishing in partnership with Difference Press. Morgan James is a trademark of Morgan James, LLC. www.MorganJamesPublishing.com

ISBN 978-1-63195-104-6 paperback
ISBN 978-1-63195-105-3 eBook
ISBN 978-1-63195-106-0 audio
Library of Congress Control Number: 2020904493

Cover Design Concept:
Nakita Duncan

Cover Design:
Megan Whitney, Creative Ninja Designs,
megan@creativeninjadesigns.com

Editor:
Cory Hott

Book Coaching:
The Author Incubator

Morgan James is a proud partner of Habitat for Humanity Peninsula and Greater Williamsburg. Partners in building since 2006.

Get involved today! Visit
www.MorganJamesBuilds.com

To Bernie, my beloved husband,
who is at times as patient as a saint.
Thank you for all the big and little ways
you've helped me to become my best self.

Table of Contents

Foreword

Look at your hands right now. Seriously. Look at them. They are fashioned to hold things. Right now, your hands are very likely holding the answers that you've long sought. Perhaps the key to the questions you've longed for. As Charlie Jones once said, "Where you'll be five years from now will be determined by the people you meet, the choices you make and the books that you'll read." Better choices are made by gaining knowledge and wisdom. This book is going to be not just 'one of the most amazing journeys' you've taken through the pages that follow; it will quite likely be the most important one you'll ever embark upon.

Sometimes, you just need someone to talk to. Someone who knows where you are or has been where you are now. You need someone who has felt the pain of a life that hasn't turned out as you'd dreamed.

When we are young, we have dreams about love, family, success and more. We have that deep sense that 'someday, I'll be extremely happy.' You, as a woman, might have thought, "I'll meet him. He'll know my needs. He'll understand who I really am. And he will fill every crevice of my soul with healing and love." However, the white picket fence seems to be no more than a taunting, teasing and cruel promise and vague hope.

What happened? Why didn't I get what I dreamed of? Why am 'I' so unlucky? Why am I so miserable, depressed and crushed in my heart?

The reality of life is, things don't go the way we'd hoped. It isn't just you, even though I know you may feel alone, unwanted and devastated. Most people face their own 'dark night of the soul.'

When I was a kid and things didn't go as expected, or they turned out to be a total disaster, my grandpa used to say, "Michael, remember. The earth is made of dirt." Grandma would fire back another quip, "And YOU are made from dirt." Even the ancient scriptures say, "In this world, you will have tribulation."

When life is spiraling out of control and it seems that all of your friends have abandoned you, there is still hope. To find that hope, I suggest that you read every word of this book. Kathryn has been where you are and perhaps even worse. She candidly opens her heart and her story to give you that hope. Not only does she inspire, but, she informs you, step-by-step, in answering your questions.

I see you sitting there asking yourself or perhaps whispering a prayer saying, "What do I do now?"

Listen to Kathryn. I know her. I'm not just someone who she's asked to write these words that I'm saying now. I know her well. She's real. This book is her. This book is you. She unravels the mystery for you in understanding where you are, what you feel and where to go from here.

I heard a man say once, 'When you buy a book, you aren't paying for paper, glue and ink. You are buying a person's life.' In this book, you aren't just holding in your hands Kathryn's life, but, you are holding the essence of her soul. She tells you her struggles as pure and as raw as they've been. You'll identify with her every step of the journey. Not only that, you'll learn how to get from where you are now to where you truly want to be.

Kathryn will take you by the hand and gently and lovingly walk with you. Not only will she show you the way to go, but, as you make this book your close companion, she'll be with you all of the way. In these pages, she becomes your best friend, your loving guide, your confident mentor, your wise counselor and more. You'll feel her warm touch as she wraps her words around your soul. Please don't just read this book. Absorb it into your own essence. Feel the pain and let these pages heal your spirit and follow her guidance.

Michael Murphy
Author of *Powerful Attitudes*
Zhengzhou, Henan, China

Chapter 1
How Did You Get Here?

*L*iking someone that you don't like is near impossible. No amount of love can make you like behavior that you don't like. Even if it is explained to you and even if you understand why your husband does what he does. At best, you can have compassion, tolerance, and patience, but that doesn't mean you ever like their behavior. Living with a spouse you do not like is living in discontent. You are sucked into a never-ending competition of proving each other wrong because your goal is to change them or ignore them, neither of which breeds harmony.

Forty-one percent of first marriages end in divorce.
Sixty percent of second marriages end in divorce.
Seventy-three percent of third marriages end in divorce.
In America, a divorce happens every thirteen seconds.
America has the sixth highest rate of divorce in the world.[1]

1

Divorce courts and divorced families are full of painful stories. That your love turned to bitterness or vengeance or sadness or was withdrawn means it was not unconditional love, but rather desire. You were full of expectations. When those expectations were not met, you were disappointed and felt betrayed. That kind of love is capricious, volatile, vacillating, fitful and irregular. In a word, it is fickle. It changes its loyalty, interest and affection frequently. That low level of love does more harm than good. It is the road to suffering.

The end of a marriage is devastating for months or years. Divorce is a kind of death. It is the end of a lifetime of plans together, of dreams of being together forever, and of you being a wife. Contemplating a life alone is so divisive that it increases the already fractious upheaval in your home. Debating whether to break up a family is giving yourself permission to break a sacred trust. There are immediate and long-term repercussions.

Different people bring out different sides of you. Humans are reactive creatures. A smile elevates your mood whereas harsh words plummet your mood. Most people assign points, often unconsciously, adding points for endearing behavior and subtracting points for annoying behavior. When the balance in a marriage tips to where there are more negative points, intervention is needed.

Most relationships need constant repair to heal the upsets, confusions, misunderstandings, disappointments, or lack of politeness. Ever notice that you treat your husband and/or are treated by him worse than you treat most everyone else? Do you catch yourself being your worst self around him? Often couples snap at each other in a way they would never do to a stranger.

Stress causes discord. Discord causes disunity. It is common to blame external events for causing your upset when in fact stress is an internal reaction; it is the way you interpret what is happening. In a word, it is your attitude that determines your reaction. A different woman would handle your husband differently, and thus, have an entirely different marriage with him.

Your attitude determines whether you see your husband as pathetic or funny. Your positionality makes him a helpmate or a hindrance. At a cellular level, the way you choose determines whether endorphins or stress hormones flood your body.

Endorphins relieve pain or stress and boost happiness, as happens when working together and building a relationship. This is called an anabolic reaction, when small molecules combine into larger ones. "Runner's high" is well-known to athletes as feeling great even though expending lots of energy. The general public better knows the experience of laughing so hard your sides hurt and you're exhausted, but you feel great.

Why be calm when you can panic?

Adrenaline and stress hormones are catabolic hormones, meaning they break down muscle. While initially enabling you to be able to contend with a problem, when perpetuated they lead to burnout. They exhaust a marriage. They prevent a marriage from having harmony. The problem is that adrenaline is highly addictive. It is a chemical the body makes when you are frightened and feel you must fight or flee. It happens without conscious thought.

Someone who is easily offended, who takes everything personally even if it was meant as a joke, who feels unwanted when not included, and who feels unloved when not adored, is a person who is hard to live with. These people turn compliments into criticism. They attack, they sulk, they shut down. You feel like you must walk on eggshells around them. It takes a saint to live with them. If you were the saint in the marriage, no wonder you feel exhausted, depleted, confused and angry. If both you and your husband easily get upset, communication is near impossible and often only causes more friction.

Panicking is a learned response. It is a desperate attempt to regain control when you feel out of control. However, the more you hold your breath, the more the panic escalates. Thus it is imperative to learn better, healthier, more peaceful ways to respond to frustration and emergencies. This book teaches fast and easy ways to break bad habits. If you're reading this book, then you've probably tried lots of ideas, but you are still unhappy and looking for an answer to your prayers. You need to build new bridges to save your marriage.

The problem is your ego, that part of you that feels entitled to worrying, grieving, getting angry and blaming your husband. There is a secret pleasure to being a martyr. You believe you are sacrificing when in fact you are forfeiting control, abandoning your job to nurture and protect your husband and family, imposing on them to take care of you, or else you'll die.

Cowing is the unseen way of bullying others into doing what you want. Your glare intimidates your husband more than complaining. He lives to make you happy. His world rises with your smile and sets when you frown. Husbands are little boys yearning for approval. You are not just a wife. You have to mother him, too. You have to teach him how to please you. Too often women misunderstand their role to thinking that they have to please their husband, when in fact, the only reason the man gets upset is because he thinks he displeased you. Cowing robs confidence; it is saying, "Do as I say, not as I do." It is manipulative. It is a dictator disguised as a dove. To stop this backdoor approach is to become authentic. To say what you mean builds trust and closeness. When you are clear and kind, your husband knows what you want. You lead by example, you show him how by staying calm, everyone gets what they want. To give up being a victim is to stop pretending that you are weak.

Think of the short list. This list is read at funerals, lauding the achievements of the deceased. What would it be like to view your husband with the short list of what you like about him? Admittedly, that would eliminate a lot of gossip and resentment. You'd have to find other topics to rant about rather than the latest, most annoying thing your husband did.

Resenting your husband is a way to vindicate yourself. The worse he is, the more you feel justified to be angry. The angrier you are, the more justified you feel to be uncooperative, moody, or withdraw your affection from him. Or to punish him. If you can prove him wrong, then you prove yourself right. Seriously? Is life ever that simple? You ask questions such as, "What's wrong with him?" or "What's his problem?" But are these the best questions you could ask? Do they promote well-being and harmony?

You want a happy relationship. You want to be respected and adored. At a minimum, you want to be treated civilly and have a helpmate. It's a bonus if your husband makes you laugh, but every relationship is like the weather. Thus, some relationships have sunnier days and others get more storms.

Every time you withdraw your positive influence, you resign from caring. In a word, you desert your husband. You stop being his helpmate. You stop being his protector. You withdraw your affection and loyalty. You become an "I" and are as separate as an island. Your health diminishes. This is God waving a red flag to wake you up from your apathy. This is your body begging you to stop destroying yourself, to give up being sad, mad, confused, overwhelmed, bitter, deceived and hopeless. It is your body begging you to embrace emotions which heal, such as compassion for yourself and others, forgiving yourself and others, and understanding that unless all benefit, no one benefits.

But what do you do when your spouse creates so many problems that he wears you down? What do you do when you've tried every good idea you can think of—counseling, following the advice of friends and family—and are at your wit's end?

Is divorce the solution? It is one solution.

Are there any other solutions that would bring peace into your life? Yes. This book teaches how to become so calm that you interact differently with your husband. You stop being adversaries and learn how to become teammates. You learn how to calm yourself when overwhelmed. You learn how to turn a miserable marriage into a happy marriage. Or, from a calm place, you get clear that your differences are irreconcilable and develop the grace of how to have an amicable divorce.

Relationships at the beginning are full of wonder and promise. Everyone is on their best behavior. It's a time of delight and discovery, excitement and anticipation, and lust and yearning. All you can think about is him. You take extra care to groom yourself, plan outings to spend time getting to know each other, listen attentively, and ask intimate and silly questions eager to know his favorite food, music, sport, color, restaurant, and dessert.

Newly in love, you had hopes and dreams of a lifetime of happiness together, and then reality hit. Resentments, disappointments, and misunderstandings weighed you down until you no longer recognized yourself. You married with blinders on. You feel like you could have coined the saying, "Love is blind." The confident, expectant girl who excitedly married her childhood sweetheart aged into a tired, aggrieved woman who is fed up and not sure where to turn. You know that God hasn't forgotten you, that he walks alongside you, but you are having trouble hearing him. You want help, you need help, and buying this book is your first step upon a journey to save your marriage or to discern if God wants you to divorce.

I disagree that the morals of society are declining. Up until a hundred years ago, many men were on their third wife by the time they were forty due to women dying in childbirth or from disease or injury. Because so many died at a young age, and also because times were harder, they literally needed each other to grow crops and raise livestock, or fight the British or the Indians, or journey out West, or tend the homestead while the husband mined for gold, and consequently divorce was not common. In addition, women had no legal rights and lost everything including their kids in a divorce. These circumstances probably kept many women from seeking a divorce in order to stay with their children.

Two thousand years ago, gladiators killed men and they called it sport. Spectators paid money to watch men kill men. A woman raped outside the city walls was thought to get what she deserved for going out alone. Today we call these crimes. Women today have the right to vote, own property, have their own bank accounts, and can file for divorce and win custody of their children. Women can work and can pay for daycare. Women are more independent today.

Why do you stay in a bad relationship?

- Because you think this is as good as it gets.
- Because you don't think you deserve any better.
- Because you hope things will improve.
- Because you made a vow to stay "in sickness and in health, in good times and bad times, and for better or for worse."

If divorcing is an unbearable shame to you, it does not feel like an option. Divorcing is to admit you made a mistake. You've survived in the marriage until now, so you expect to be able to continue surviving. You know how to contend with this set of problems whereas divorcing creates new problems that might be worse. But what if you want and expect more out of life than just surviving? What if your marriage could improve?

Lavinia was thirty-eight, the mother of three kids, ages three, nine, and twelve. She was a nurse and worked full-time at a hospital. She married her high school sweetheart and while it was never an easy marriage, his drinking bouts had intensified. His constantly changing jobs and increasingly long gaps in between jobs made her feel like a single mom even though married. She was the main breadwinner and did ninety-eight percent of the parenting. However, she was devoutly religious and opposed to divorce.

She was discouraged, overwhelmed, and didn't know what to do.

She prayed several times a day for guidance, strength and courage. Was her husband acting out so that she would kick him out? Did God want her to divorce? Was there a way to save her marriage? These thoughts looped like a stuck record and kept her awake at night. She asked advice from ministers, friends and family, and an MFCC (Marriage, Family and Child Counseling licensed therapist). Each had different opinions.

Divorce causes so many unforeseen problems and divides a family. However, sometimes it is still the best option. But too often your being upset blinds you from seeing solutions. When upset, you slam doors shut, metaphorically and literally. By calming down, doors open in unexpected and wondrous ways, and once again you can hear God speak. What you decide to do is your business and God's business.

"Defense is the first act of war."
— **Byron Katie**

You feel justified to defend yourself. You feel entitled to be indignant when slighted or misunderstood. But it takes two to fight. Each defense escalates a fight. Often the fight builds to where you're in a verbal boxing match. The longer the fight persists, the bloodier emotionally it gets. In extreme cases, real blood is shed.

Someone wise said, "Don't poop where you sleep." Meaning the more you disrespect your husband, the more you destroy your sacred place. Your home is supposed to be a cathedral of love and honor. But what do you do when the storms are inside the house and you find yourself not wanting to go home? Change has to happen.

Changing yourself is hard. Changing your husband is near impossible. Yet, when you truly change, those around you change. But it doesn't work to change while expecting him to change. That's like saying, "I'll be different, if you'll be different," and not telling him that this is the new agreement. Which usually sets everyone up for failure.

Bad relationships are like cancer. They suck your energy. Ultimately it is your job to take care of yourself first, in the same way that on an airplane adults put their own mask on before putting on their child's oxygen mask.

What is it costing you to stay in this relationship?

What is the worst-case scenario if you stay and things don't change?

What is the worst-case scenario if you divorce?

What if there was a way to determine whether divorce is your best solution?

"Out of a mountain of despair comes a stone of hope."
– Martin Luther King

Chapter 2

China and Beyond

I'm happily married, but this is my third marriage. I'm grateful that a six-year relationship didn't make it to the alter because I walked out on that man, too. Each of these men were hard-working, good providers, generous and adored me. I cherished and to this day still love each of them, but at some point stopped liking them, and it felt necessary to say goodbye.

In my first marriage, I truly thought I was happily married. I just wanted to commit suicide 6,000 times. I'd be driving along, feeling fine, when suddenly I'd have the urge to yank the wheel into a ditch. No amount of psychotherapy stopped the urge to drive off a cliff. It took an out-of-body suicide before I realized I wanted out of my marriage.

After an argument with my husband, I snatched up my keys. Hurrying through the kitchen, I glanced out the window to take one last look at my daughters, ages four and twelve, playing in the backyard. Peace enveloped me, and I surrendered my ego to be with God. Time stopped. Meaning my body stayed in the kitchen, my feet glued to the floor, but my mind experienced careening off a cliff in my white Mazda. This vision was as real as though it happened. Free-falling, an inner voice spoke with clear resolve, "Anything—divorce—is better than this."

Suddenly I wanted to live and frantically worked to unlatch the safety belt, desperate to jump free of the car. The next second, I was back in my kitchen. While my body had not left the kitchen, my soul had dissociated from my body and God had intervened.

Shaken, I went for a drive to process what had happened, but without the goal of suicide. The vision lasted less than a minute, yet I was forever changed. It would be the last time I used suicide as a solution to end pain.

I asked for a divorce.

I dated a psychologist for six years. It was wonderful until it wasn't. When he didn't want to spend time with me, make love, go for hikes or bike rides or out to eat, I ended the romance. We had reconciled thirty times, but when I saw this as an endless pattern of him only eager to be with me when we weren't together—but as a couple had little time or interest or even a smile for me—I felt neglected and moved on.

I dated and married a banker. It felt like my heart grew bigger with each relationship, that a new bedroom was created for each man and was sealed when the relationship ended. When problems started after our wedding, I called my ex-boyfriend for advice. "I can't believe I'm going to help you keep your marriage," but he patiently and generously did. His counsel always calmed me down and gave new insight of how to contend with difficult situations. I called him often, for many problems arose with this new husband's kids who lived with us, his son, sixteen, and his daughter, nineteen. Before joining this family, I had thought I liked kids. They proved me wrong. Being a stepmom is the hardest task in the world. Anything you do that they don't like brands you as the evil stepmother.

Until then, I had thought mothering was the easiest, greatest, most fun job in the world. My daughters had never caused me upheaval. I rarely said no, but when I did, they knew it wasn't up for discussion, that my no was final. To be challenged by my husband's kids felt like impudence. It got so awkward that his daughter moved to her mother's house. Since my husband had been best friends with his daughter at the time we started dating, I suggested they start meeting for lunch without me. From that point on, their lunches became a highlight of their week.

That second marriage was the best and the worst, and ultimately wore me out. Depression set in. I could no longer handle being a Rolfer and developed vending routes for a charity. Besieged with shame, fear, and anger, I looked twenty years older. Pepsi and chocolate became my best friends. I spent most days not interacting with people, and read or played word games. When my youngest went away to university, the house seemed too big and too empty.

My hormones dipped so low that I went on hormone replacement therapy. I felt good enough to look for a part-time job in an office. The internet made it easy to apply online. Almost one hundred applications later and after only one interview, I read an ad to teach English in China. "I'd love to do that! Oh wait, I have a husband."

I told myself no, yet yearned to go. Being self-employed since age nineteen, I didn't have any supervisors to write letters of recommendation, so I asked two close friends, both professionals, who wouldn't think me crazy. When I got their recommendations, they described the person I was before the marriage. Finally, I decided I had to go to China if only to see if I could once again become that person who loved life, people, her job, and was on good terms with most everyone.

Freud Described Depression as Anger Turned Inward

Overnight, I had energy, enthusiasm, and a future which made sense to me. No longer was it hard to walk up a flight of stairs nor did I fill my day playing games on the computer. Packing up my office so that my stepson could move back in with us, I opened an old journal and saw my list of one hundred things I wanted to do before I died. Going to China was listed first. I was surprised. I didn't remember writing that two years before. I wondered if hearing my grandma say whenever life got frustrating, "I just want to get on a slow boat to China," made China seem a safe place.

My family and friends varied greatly in their reaction. My daughters were supportive and not surprised. Whereas my dad asked bewildered, "What kind of person does that?" A little bit embarrassed, I said, "Me." A relative asked, "Aren't you kind of old to go?" "Not getting any younger," I retorted. My path delighted new acquaintances, but in fairness, to them I was Kathryn-going-to-China. As soon as they met me, they knew I was leaving, so I was not abandoning them, I was just someone interesting.

The day I left, I looked out over the Pacific Ocean from our deck, the view as jaw-dropping gorgeous as the first day I saw it. Santa Cruz Island stood in sharp relief against the blue sea, the barren patches shone gold, the trees so clear you could almost count them. The city of Santa Barbara looked quaint with its red tile roofs nestled in greenery. The harbor looked like a postcard and remains the cutest harbor I've ever seen, big enough to hold cruise ships and small enough to be a short walk to your boat. I stared long to etch the view into memory and whispered, "I give up this view to see one thousand more."

Choosing One Path Eliminates Others

Deciding to adventure to China was the most controversial and, in many people's opinion, craziest decision of my life. I was fifty-two. Two years earlier, I had wanted to get a divorce on the grounds that I didn't like who I had become. However, I realized I wasn't strong enough to take care of myself and thus had to get stronger, to leave or to stay.

I went to China fully expecting to return at the end of the school year, but when learned I might have a pituitary tumor, I decided that if I had two months to live or twenty years, I didn't want to fight anymore and asked for a divorce. We had fought most every day, but from the moment I asked for a divorce, we never fought again and divorced amicably.

I liked China so much that I stayed for eight years. I met and married a Canadian colleague. When we retired from China, moving to Canada was the hardest move of my life, probably because I couldn't work until I got permanent residency, a process that took two years.

Giving up teaching in China turned me inside out. Overwhelmed, I needed the help of a life coach to navigate this transition. I'd had a dozen careers and moved thirty times—as well as lived in America, Germany, Brazil and China—yet those changes seemed like kindergarten compared to moving to Nova Scotia. I didn't know it was a province of Canada until I met my husband.

I felt bereft, like my identity had been stripped away. Without China, I was no longer cool or interesting. I was a has-been. My future loomed as endless days of cooking, cleaning and watching television. I hoped love would be enough, but once again it wasn't. I cooked more for my husband than for my kids when they lived at home, sometimes three meals a day, and I joked it was just a phase. My contentment teaching tenth graders in China at a prestigious high school made banal jobs like cooking a little bit fun.

Who was I without my job? English teachers in Zhengzhou were treated like celebrities. In Canada, I was a nobody, literally, just an expat who married a Canadian. People changed when they found out I was an American, like they had to convince me that Canada was better, or explain how it was different. For example, "We don't have guns like you do."

Not every day was easy or fun working in China. There were days I wanted to teleport back, especially when my daughters were sick. They were successful adults, but I wanted to be there to mother them back to health. I felt like a mom gone rogue. However, it assuaged my guilt that my daughters thrived in my absence. I had gone to China expecting to stay one year, but each year I signed up for another year. Working in China was always a temporary assignment, whereas moving to Nova Scotia was for the rest of my life.

Add to that my best friends stayed in China. They envied my life of leisure; I envied their having a job they loved. My husband has more than one hundred relatives living in Nova Scotia, all who welcomed me with open arms and friendship, and whom I like and adore, however the dynamics between my husband and I changed. We were no longer banded as two ex-pats on the other side of the world who adventured other countries. He was home, whereas I was still an ex-pat.

He liked retirement; I did not. I chafed to be unemployed. However, it made sense to live in Nova Scotia. He owned a home. The cost of living was cheaper. Medical care was inexpensive. However, my daughters lived in California, five thousand miles away. If health or finances precluded my traveling to see them, it meant seeing them at most once a year. What if my husband got sick, and I couldn't leave? Depression swirled like a vortex and threatened to drown me in regret for my life decisions.

Crying was my sport and hobby. I dashed to bathrooms like battling Montezuma's Revenge, for it's always worked best for me to grieve alone. And it was grieving. I loved teaching in China. I applied for volunteer jobs, but even they wanted a police criminal check, letters of recommendation, a resume, pages of paperwork, and three interviews to clean out litter boxes in an animal hospital.

Hot showers became my best friend and covered up the noise of sobbing. I felt a bit desperate, confused, and surprised at my histrionics. I thought I'd prepared myself well for this new chapter of my life; I'd researched and listed three pages of activities and clubs to get involved with, and yet the tears hit like a tsunami.

I hid my tears from my husband as best I could, but I was not fun to live with. Everything that had worked in the past did not lift my spirits, so I went in search of new ways to thrive. One night getting into bed, tears climbed my throat, and I resolved, "No, I will give it one year." Meaning I would not cry anymore, for it takes time to make new friends, and settle into a new country. The tears evaporated.

That decision shifted my focus to stop bemoaning the past and start living in the present. I had an epiphany: I had to make Canada more wonderful and more exciting than China or else I would resent my husband forever. I hired editors to help me finish a book started before going to China. The book morphed into something grander than it began. The editors culled out the best of me. They inspired me to reveal my shame, sharing feelings I'd never articulated. I had a new identity: I was a serious author.

The future loomed more exciting than China, especially the prospect of becoming a motivational speaker. Teaching joy brings me joy. Traveling is one of my favorite pastimes. Happy with my future, I embrace life with anticipation and expectation. I've always loved the forests and lakes of Nova Scotia, but now it feels like home.

Coaching you to determine whether divorce is right for you is passing forward what I have learned. There are always tradeoffs to whatever you decide. This book helps you make those decisions with grace and compassion.

Chapter 3

You Are Awesome

*T*o make your marriage easier requires going on a journey of self-discovery. Therefore, the essential steps are segmented into manageable chunks using the acronym J.O.U.R.N.E.Y. This journey is designed to help whatever stage you in: (1) frustrated and seeking how to bring harmony to your marriage; (2) if you are contemplating divorce or separation; (3) are in the midst of divorcing; and (4) if you are already divorced. Each chapter builds upon the last, however, you can read them in any order.

J = Joy Takes Guts
O = Overwhelm versus Opportunity
U = Understanding Your Authentic Self
R = Reinvent Yourself into Someone You Admire
N = New Skills to Make Your Journey Easier
E = Emancipation from Bad Habits
Y = You Love Your Decision

You can live a long time on hope. But at some point, hope isn't enough and you need results. This is a results-oriented book to mentor you through the difficult process of deciding if divorce is right for you. Contemplating divorce begins a journey that ultimately improves your life, or fills you with regret or anger. Your life must be far better off emotionally after your divorce or else what was the point of going through with it?

All you need to attain the marriage you want is the patience and courage to learn new skills, the focus and faith of prayer to trust that changing you is your only salvation, and surrendering whatever blocks you from letting go of negative thoughts. This book teaches ways to make your journey easier. In this book you will find:

- Ways to assess what is most bothering you (and it probably isn't what you think).
- How to find solutions.
- Ways to assess what you most need from your husband.
- Ways to empower you to take better care of yourself.
- Ways to measure whether things are getting better.
- Ways to get clarity and understanding about your marriage.
- Ways to bring harmony into your home.

Divorce or contemplating divorce is usually painful, complicated, and requires answering hard questions. You didn't marry with the intention or expectation to divorce, so even if you are the one who wanted it, there is grief. There is loss. There is upheaval. Divorce is the death of a marriage. Traditions end. People leave. Friends take sides. Your world turns upside down. It takes time to learn how to do life without your husband, how to sleep alone, and how to heal wounds. It means figuring out how to get along with someone you no longer want to live with, or who no longer wants to live with you.

Pain leaves scars. If you have children, it means learning how to be a single parent, cooperating with your ex on holidays and vacations, figuring out custody, figuring out what to tell your kids, how to not talk badly about your ex in front of the kids, and dealing with your ex-laws.

The purpose of this book is to make this transition easier, to minimize the pain and conflict, to gain clarity before making difficult decisions, and ultimately to help you to take good care of yourself.

Journeys mean navigating uncharted territory, raw with emotion, and you need a guide to show you the way, a map from someone who has been through divorce so knows those pitfalls and who also figured out how to be happily married. This journey requires courage. It means asking questions that you find difficult to ask and to answer, or are not yet ready to answer, or don't know what to ask. This book is like a beacon that sheds light to safe harbors to recuperate when things don't go as you planned.

Courage does not mean that you are not afraid, but rather that you have the mental strength to face hardship, the determination to try your best, and the willingness to persevere even when it hurts. Courage is like understanding how magic tricks work. No longer are you bamboozled by the inequities of life or the insanity of people. The majority of people are negative, too blind to see the miracles that abound every day and everywhere, including in their own lives. Courage is not stopping until you get the results you seek.

J = Joy Takes Guts

Debating whether to stay in a marriage or to leave is an emotional journey. Whichever way you choose affects your life and the lives of your family. This chapter explains emotions. It is imperative to know how life-destroying emotions such as shame, grief, apathy, guilt, fear, anger, and pride increase tension and prolong pain. In contrast, life-supporting emotions such as courage and willingness build bridges over heartache. What most people call love isn't love. It is desire, lust, dependency, and expectation. True love is unconditional, a high state of consciousness, wherein there is no right or wrong. Neither party is good or bad. There are no regrets, no blame, no shame, no anger, no defensiveness, only compassion.

This chapter teaches how to ask better questions. Questions that are void of blame encourage cooperation and build harmony. Too often, out of spite or anger or hurt or vengeance, couples turn a squall into a hurricane. Focusing on what is important and what needs to change brings clarity. Clarity brings resolution. Resolution brings harmony. Harmony brings peace. Thus, clarity is the turning point of dispelling confusion and knowing which steps to take to move toward reconciliation. Clarity makes building a new life separate from your husband an easier path. Empowered people have the ability to learn new skills.

O = Overwhelm versus Opportunity

It's easy to blame others for your upsets, disappointments, and frustrations. Yet, to the degree that you do, you become a victim. You forfeit your power and let others manipulate you. You even stop asserting yourself in the hope of keeping the peace.

This chapter explains how shame undermines your confidence, how depression is anger turned inwards, and how it takes courage to change. Whether you want to save your marriage or end it, you need new skills and understanding of how to navigate the storm of emotions that often result before, during, and after divorcing.

U = Understanding Your Authentic Self

Marriage is hard and usually a series of compromises. To figure out whether to stay in your marriage or end it, you need clarity. Clarity only comes in moments of calm. This chapter teaches ways to find calm while in the midst of upheaval. What you learn in this chapter is useful for the rest of your life, whether you choose to work things out or decide it's in everyone's best interest to divorce. It doesn't matter who asked for the divorce initially. In the end, both parties signed the papers, meaning both parties publicly declared that this is what they wanted.

Sometimes you choose things that don't feel good or make sense, but seem necessary and right. However, it can take months or even years to see the wisdom of your choice. This chapter teaches how to find clarity before making tough decisions. Deciding what you want is the hardest part. After that, it's just logistics.

R = Reinvent Yourself into Someone You Admire

Emotions wear you down. Life can become a roller coaster of turns, loops, and spirals. Anger, guilt, grief, shame, fear, and pride destroy you and harm your family. Yet, this is the arena where most people live. Most people don't know there are better options. Most people are too invested in being right, and refuse to calm down and gain perspective.

Courage is the first rung of the emotions that support life. Courage is when you begin to gain clarity. Clarity is seeing options that work for both you and your husband. Clarity is seeing new solutions to old problems. Taking full responsibility for your life is perhaps the hardest transformation to master. It's not how you were raised, not what you were taught in school, not what your government demonstrates, nor what the news propagates. Most people believe it's always someone else's fault.

Humans are reactive creatures. To gain control over your reactions is to master life. To see the knee-jerk reaction before doing it—and choose not to do it, but instead respond in a way that supports life—is a skill that creates miracles. Just trying to learn this skill will improve the quality of your life. It could save your marriage or make divorce the springboard of a new and wonderful life.

N = New Skills to Make Your Journey Easier

Marriages that are in the throes of contemplating divorce, or have just ended it, are usually at their worst. Getting married seemed a good idea, but now feels like a nightmare. Accusations and untruths fly like arrows wounding you and your husband, and justify why you left or want out. Exaggerations distort reality. Defending and explaining parlay until both you and your husband are battle-worn and weary.

Most couples are best friends when they get married, so to slide down into the malcontent of hating each other, of avoiding your husband to protect yourself, of wishing you'd never see or hear from him again, of thinking you were crazy and made a mistake, is to turn love into regret.

Thus, it is imperative to rise above the life-destroying emotions to save yourself and your children. Hope feels good, but fizzles out. Results validate progress. Measurable progress must be made at frequent intervals to sustain moments of doubt.

E = Emancipation from Bad Habits

Negative thoughts weigh you down. They are a luxury you cannot afford. They are looking at what's wrong with life instead of what is good. Anytime you are sad or mad you are resisting life rather than embracing it. You can't bring harmony into your marriage or your life by using force. Your level of consciousness determines your perspective and your result. Raising your level to an emotion which supports life such as courage, neutrality, willingness, acceptance, reason, love, peace, and/or enlightenment is like clearing away the dark clouds and basking in sunshine. These high level emotions are powerful enough to create miracles like saving your marriage, or bringing clarity so clear that you know God wants you to end your marriage because he has a more wondrous path planned for you.

Your job is to move beyond your ego, like dropping ballast, so you can fly far and wide, the way God intended. Your ego whines, nips, barks, bites, thinks destroying things is fun, and is hard to train. Think naughty puppy. Your ego destroys things out of boredom and curiosity. It literally doesn't know any better. You must train and discipline your ego into submission. The easiest way to do that is to raise your level of consciousness, beyond the reach of the ego. This chapter teaches several ways to ride an elevator back up to sanity, grace, and God when life turns upside down.

Y = You Love Your Decision

If you have read the book and done each exercise, you will have learned many new skills and raised your level of consciousness up to emotions that support life. You will have gotten clarity about whether divorce is right for you. You will be at peace with this decision. You will feel connected to God, and know you have his blessing. You will be excited about your future, and feel confident that you can handle whatever new challenges come along.

To reinvent yourself into someone you admire, you have to grow and shed many skins. Like a caterpillar, at first the process is slow and arduous. However, each new skill increases your level of consciousness and makes the old skin too tight. Thus, you slough off that one, expand your consciousness as big as possible, and grow a bigger awareness. The end result is someone you hardly recognize, but someone you can trust. You have a plan for your future, and a map that makes sense. You are your own hero.

Unless your life is better after divorcing—or choosing to stay together—you will resent everybody including yourself. Resentment comes from feeling you made the wrong choice. You want to succeed, be happy, and thrive. Yet, thriving is only possible when exercising life-supporting emotions such as courage, willingness, neutrality, and wisdom. It takes time to break old habits. It takes effort to learn new skills. It takes courage to change.

Think of this book as your new best friend.

You can read the chapters in any order. You can do the exercises, activities, and meditations in any order. Do whatever is easiest, or most appealing, or whatever you most need right now. Sometimes what worked yesterday doesn't work today, and what worked for one person doesn't work for you, therefore I've included numerous ways to calm down to get the clarity you need, to know what you need to do.

After you read this book, my biggest hope is that you have the results that you desire. However, if feel you need or want more help, you can reach out by emailing me at KathrynMacIntyreJOY@gmail.com.

Chapter 4

J = Joy Takes Guts

*T*his chapter provides the groundwork needed to gain clarity. Clarity only comes in moments of calm. Upsets are like storms with thunder and lightning. Calm is the blue skies and sunshine, always there, but hidden by the storm. To successfully make this journey, you need to understand the scientific calibrations of emotions. The activities, exercises and meditations in this chapter are fast ways to get clear about what is bothering you. More importantly, they teach you new ways to increase calm and well-being.

Is divorce your best solution? Might there be an even better solution? These thoughts can keep you awake night after night, circling with the pros and cons until confusion and weariness make you unsure of which way to go. First you need to ask better questions. In order to ask better questions, you need to understand how emotions work.

Dr. David Hawkins was an internationally renowned psychiatrist, lecturer and expert in human consciousness who wrote a compelling book entitled Power vs. Force. In it, he explains how your level of consciousness affects you.

In his map of consciousness, he explains how the overall average level of human consciousness stands at 207, just above the base level of 200. It is only in recent centuries that mankind has shifted consciousness from the level of force to power.

What is more, just fifteen percent of the world's population is above the critical level of 200. That fifteen percent has the weight to counterbalance the negativity of the remaining eighty-five percent of the world's population. Were it not for these counterbalances, mankind would self-destruct out of the sheer mass of negativity.

Hawkins' hierarchy goes up to one thousand, the highest level of human consciousness. He believed that the only people to have achieved one thousand were Lord Jesus Christ, Lord Buddha, and Lord Krishna. He found that in the mid-seventies the planet as a whole averaged a level of consciousness of just over two hundred, meaning that the planet shifted into supporting life, which was of paramount importance since technology had advanced to where it could destroy the entire planet.

Hawkins separated the chart into two parts. The bottom half are emotions that destroy life. Shame is the lowest level of consciousness and calibrates at a mere twenty out of one thousand. The top half are emotions that support life. While you can slide up and down the scale, there is usually a predominant state which is your "normal." That you're reading this book means you're probably at least at the level of courage, which calibrates at two hundred.

Hawkins found that the lower, life-destroying, emotions use force whereas the higher, life-supporting emotions, use power. Think of forcing yourself to do something that you don't want to do. It's hard, takes effort, and is like pushing something heavy uphill. Compare that to utilizing the power of the universe, and doing the same task with ease. Notice how the latter has no judgment, no resistance, no strenuous effort, and no resentment. While Hawkins began his professional life as an agnostic, a near-death experience made him a devout believer.

"I fell ill with a progressive, fatal illness that did not respond to any treatments available. By age 38, I was in extremis and knew I was about to die. I didn't care about the body, but my spirit was in a state of extreme anguish and despair. As the final moment approached, the thought flashed through my mind, 'What if there is a God?' So I called out in prayer, 'If there is a God, I ask him to help me now.' I surrendered to whatever God there might be and went into oblivion. When I awoke, a transformation of such enormity had taken place that I was struck with awe.

"The person I had been no longer existed. There was no personal self or ego. Only an Infinite Presence of such unlimited power that it was all that was. This Presence replaced what had been 'me,' and the body and its actions were controlled solely by the Infinite Will of the Presence. The world was illuminated by the clarity of an Infinite Oneness that expressed itself as all things revealed in their infinite beauty and perfection."

– **David R. Hawkins**, *Power vs. Force*

Hawkins summarized the levels of consciousness as a scale, emotion, process, and life-view associated with each level. Because your emotions fluctuate, and more importantly because the life-destroying emotions create havoc in your life and especially in your marriage, I go over them in detail. Hawkins created the labels. The descriptions are based on his findings, but slanted with my experience. Hawkins deemed this a logarithmic scale, meaning at the higher levels there are significantly fewer people. Think pyramid. More people are at the lower energy fields than at the higher energy fields. Thus, to increase to a higher level will create such change in your life that it changes all those around you. If you want to save your marriage, or build a new and better life after divorcing, the fastest way to do so is to increase your level of consciousness.

The following descriptions are adopted from Hawkins' levels of consciousness and Steve Pavlina's blog (https://www.stevepavlina.com/blog/2005/04/levels-of-consciousness/).

The Ego: Emotions That Destroy Life

Shame—Humiliation/Elimination/Miserable

Self-hatred. Feels like you don't deserve the air you breathe and should kill or punish yourself. Or you may feel the urge to kill or punish others. The level of serial killers and people who cut themselves. Cutting creates physical pain which is easier to deal with than emotional pain. Physical pain is tangible. Emotional pain is abstract and psychological.

Guilt—Blame/Destruction/Condemnation (Evil)

A level above shame, but you still may think about suicide, if only to stop the overwhelming pain. You cannot forgive yourself for what you think you did wrong.

Apathy—Despair/Abdication/Hopeless

You have given up hope that life can ever get better; feel victimized, and with no control, so why even try. Numb feels better than shame or guilt.

Grief—Regret/Despondency/Tragic

Sad and overwhelmed with loss. Feel raw and easily cry. Depressed. A step above apathy for now you are rising above the numbness.

<u>Fear—Anxiety/Withdrawal/Frightening</u>

You believe the world is dangerous, often paranoid. Because easily scared, easily controlled and manipulated. The level of abusive relationships.

<u>Desire—Craving/Enslavement/Disappointing</u>

Excessive or compulsive dieting and food disorders. Addiction. Lust. Craving for attention, money, prestige, accumulation of things. Shopping disorders. Alcoholism. Drugs. Smoking. Excessive talking, bragging, bullying.

<u>Anger—Hate/Aggression/Antagonist</u>

Frustrated when disappointed. Sometimes anger can jumpstart you to higher levels such as courage, however if perpetuated, leads to hatred. Abusive relationships often pair an angry person with a person at the level of fear. Inflexible, convinced you are right. Attack without thinking about the consequences. No compassion for yourself or others.

<u>Pride—Dignity (Scorn)/Inflation/Demanding</u>

This level feels great, but is false because it is entirely dependent on external achievements, such as attaining money, fame, beauty, winning or prestige which makes it a hollow victory and vulnerable to being attacked. Racism. Nationalism. Wars emanate from this level. Narrow-minded logic. Insecure. Easily offended. Any attack on your belief is viewed as an attack on you. Easily angered if challenged. You believe things are right and wrong. Fundamentalists who believe only their beliefs are correct. Think of the Crusades. Yet, the first commandment for Christians is "Thou shall not kill." Pride mixed with fear make people want to kill before they are killed. Though this level feels good, it is a level of denial and defensiveness.

Think: U.S. Marines. At this level, people use phrases like "No pain, no gain."

While these emotions ultimately destroy life, they can be a catalyst to moving to a higher level. It is when you get stuck at that level that harm results.

Emotions That Support Life

It is not until we let go of the ego and begin to listen to a higher consciousness that we begin to truly be kind to ourselves and others.

Courage—Affirmation/Empowerment/Feasible

The first level of integrity. Life is no longer overwhelming, but instead viewed as a challenging adventure. You are willing to learn new things, take classes, try new things. Mistakes are viewed as stepping stones to mastery. You are determined to make your future better than your past.

Neutrality—Trust/Release/Satisfactory

Flexible, easy-going, unattached to opinions or beliefs. You don't feel the need to prove anything nor defend your actions or beliefs. Congenial, sociable and comfortable with people. Often self-employed. Sometimes viewed by others as complacent or lazy. While taking care of your needs, you are neither driven nor compulsive, but simply do what is necessary.

Willingness—Optimism/Intention/Hopeful

You feel secure and content. You live with the intention to improve your life and the lives of others. You expect results. You strive to do your best. You are more productive as strive to be more efficient with your time, money and resources. This is the level of willpower and self-discipline. Known as the "troopers" of society, these people are reliable, dependable and rarely complain. As students, they are serious and excel. They are easy to be around, helpful, and rarely dwell on past mistakes or reminiscing. They face the future with confidence and expectation. They are the epitome of hopeful.

Acceptance—Forgiveness/Transcendence/Harmonious

Unconditional and absolute forgiveness. Competent. Proactive. Set and achieve goals, not compulsively to attain favor with others, but to benefit mankind. You feel an integral part of the world, and thus, responsible for maintaining the health and well-being of all things. The level of the Serenity Prayer: "God grant me the courage to change the things I can, the serenity to accept the things I can't, and the wisdom to know the difference." At this level you take full responsibility for your life, and are likely to change jobs, careers, relationships or eating habits.

Reason—Understanding/Abstraction/Meaningful

You notice discrepancies in order to rectify them. You have the ability to reframe discord, nightmares and confusion into understanding, and thus, reap benefits from the insights gleaned. You strive to leave places better than you found them, for example, pick up trash and diffuse mayhem in groups. You have control over your emotions and rarely dip into the lower level emotions that create discord. You have the ability to think clearly. Think doctors and scientists. According to Hawkins, both Freud and Einstein calibrated at 499.

Love—Reverence/Revelation/Benign

Not the sentiment of love, but rather the level of unconditional love, a permanent understanding of your connectedness with all that exists, and that all are equal. Compassionate. At the level of reason, thoughts dictated behavior, and there was a tendency to over-intellectualize.

Whereas at this level, you follow your heart, and have control over your ego. You follow passionate endeavors, compelled by your conscience. Your motives are pure. You turn your life over to serving mankind. Think Gandhi and Mother Teresa. You surrender to a force greater than yourself, and you follow your quiet voice, that inner wisdom that is the voice of God. There is less need to make plans because intuition guides you. Hawkins claimed that only one out of 250 people reach this level.

Joy—Serenity/Transfiguration/Complete

Think saints and advanced spiritual teachers. Their love is so powerful that just gazing into their eyes heals pieces of your soul. You feel hugged just being around them. You feel more complete than you ever knew possible. At the same time, you are more aware of your weaknesses because you finally feel safe enough to rise above denial and show your true fallible self. People at this level live by synchronicity and intuition. They know and see visions beyond the scope of the average person. While called eccentric or crazy by people of the lower, destructive emotions of shame, blame, guilt, grief, fear, anger and especially pride, time proves their interpretations and predictions to be accurate and brilliant. They shine so brightly with light so pure that they are not trusted by the low-level masses, yet are revered by those at the level of courage or higher.

Peace—Bliss/Illumination/Perfect

Beyond ordinary experience or comprehension. Transcending body, mind and soul. Hawkins claimed that only one person in ten million reaches this level.

Enlightenment—Ineffable/Pure Consciously/Is

To surpass mind, body and soul to where the person channels divinity. The very highest level of consciousness that a human can achieve. To think about this level raises your consciousness. Hawkins believed that only three people in history achieved this level: Lord Jesus Christ, Lord Buddha and Lord Krishna.

Therefore, it is your illusions that cause problems. People of high levels of consciousness believe that there is no such thing as a problem, that it is your resistance to accepting, as well as your negative interpretation of what you perceive as happening, that causes your suffering. They see life as merely navigating between what you want and what you don't want. Every positive choice that you make, meaning every decision you make that comes from a state of courage, neutrality, willingness, acceptance, reason, love, joy, peace or enlightenment, increases the likelihood and probability of your making more positive choices. Every positive choice you make supports life and increases your level of consciousness.

How much do you add drama to your life due to boredom or curiosity? Or because you forgot you choose your reality? It takes two to squabble. It can be infuriating to be told you're wrong when you believe you are right. However, depending on your level of consciousness, you will react differently. Thus, the more often you can climb up to higher states of consciousness, the easier it will be to navigate staying in the marriage or ending it. The purpose of this book is to guide and teach easy and fast ways to elevate your mood and increase your well-being. It is helpful to assess what level of consciousness you are at right now.

1. What level are you at this moment?
2. What is the highest level you've ever achieved?
3. What's the lowest level you've experienced?
4. Assess the range that you most generally slide between.
5. On a scale of one to ten, meaning ten is the best you have ever felt in your entire life, where would you rate yourself right now?

David R. Hawkins published *Power vs. Force* in 1995. The overall level of consciousness of the book was calibrated at 850, meaning that reading his book raises your consciousness. The book got praise from around the world from scientists, presidents, business leaders, and Mother Teresa.

While Hawkins is esteemed as the international expert on human consciousness, he was not the first to link consciousness to emotions. As far back as the 6th century B.C., Lao Tzu, an ancient Chinese philosopher wrote, "The key to growth is the introduction of higher dimensions of consciousness into our awareness."[2] Lao Tzu "is believed to be the father of Chinese Taoism (a philosophy that advocates living a simple life)."[3]

Clarity Meditation

To gain clarity in making decisions.

1. Find a quiet place where you won't be interrupted.
2. Can be done sitting up or lying down.
3. Close your eyes.
4. Tighten your whole body and immediately let it go.
5. Do that a second time.
6. Take a few deep breaths, exhaling as hard as you can.
7. Allow your body to relax even more.
8. See if you can let your shoulders drop even more.
9. Imagine that everything in your life is frozen. Your marriage doesn't get any worse, but it doesn't get any better. Your money situation doesn't get any worse, but it doesn't get any better. Your health doesn't get any worse, but it doesn't get any better. Your job doesn't get any worse, but it doesn't get any better. Everything is frozen exactly as it is.

10. Notice what you're okay with if it doesn't change, and notice what wouldn't be okay with you. Go through every aspect of your life.

11. Now imagine that you have lost everything. Your husband, family, friends, health, money, job. You're going to get it all back new again, but first you lose it all.

12. Go through every aspect of your life, and notice which areas you're okay with losing, and which you're not.

13. Imagine that you have a magic wand, and can create your life to be the way you want. You can create the marriage you want, the house of your dreams, your perfect job, optimal health, abundant money, whatever you would like to create.

The point is to get clear what is bothering you, and to get clear on what you want and need.

Make a Vision Board

To map where you want to go.

Now that you know what you want, make a vision board. This can be as small as a three- by five-inch index card that you carry in your purse, or it can be the size of a sheet of paper that you hang, or bigger. The size isn't important. Putting it where you will see it often is important. The subconscious is always alert, so the more often you see words or images of your goals, the more it focuses the subconscious to work on those goals, even while you are unaware.

If you're afraid some of your goals might upset your husband, cover up those goals with other goals so that you know they are there, but are not making them public, yet. Pictures are great, but words work, too, especially when using an index card because of limited space. Cover both sides of the index card as it's easy to look at both sides.

Put the card or vision board where you will see it several times a day. Read the words out loud first thing in the morning and before bedtime. This helps the subconscious work while you're asleep.

If you've made a vision board before, but it's more than six months old, update it with whatever new goals you've made from doing the Clarity Meditation. Vision boards work because they are a visual reminder, more powerful than words.

List Your Victories

To build confidence and facilitate new victories.

Remembering your successes empowers you to have faith in yourself. You had the strength and fortitude to survive past hurdles, therefore, you probably can overcome your current difficulty. Divide your life into three equal parts. List three to five top achievements you did in each of those segments. For example, a forty-year-old would separate the segments into ages one to thirteen, fourteen to twenty-seven, twenty-eight to forty.

1. Get a piece of paper and a pen.
2. Divide the years of your life into three equal parts.
3. List up to five top achievements in each segment.

Now make a list of the top one hundred victories of your life. Be sure to go year-by-year so that you remember accomplishments that you may have forgotten. For example, when I did this exercise after reading Jack Canfield's book, *The Success Principles*, I was surprised how many accomplishments I made from ages fourteen to seventeen. I only remembered those as miserable years. That I accomplished victories despite molestations, abandonment, and my mother's death made me feel better about that time of my life.

On a scale of one to ten, meaning ten is the best you have ever felt in your entire life, where would you rate yourself right now?

Compared to the number you wrote a few pages back, is it higher?

If not, why not? What happened between then and now that lowered this number? You've just spent a long time focusing on your victories, which usually makes one feel good about themselves, so who or what intervened to make your spirits plummet?

What if the world is actually entertainment, a melodrama as farcical as you choose to make it, depending on how outraged and upset you choose to be? That is not meant to be irreverent. Devout people who function at the higher energy levels take full responsibility for their reactions, recognize upsets as judgment and choose to remain neutral. They accept and allow others to choose life as they choose, without judging them, or trying to "fix" them. They willingly let others spin in upheaval without trying to rescue them.

Rescue implies danger, fear and helplessness. Rescue implies that force is needed to extricate the person from themselves, from danger, from evil. This is the level of believing that abused women need intervention, to be rescued from their mean husbands, when in truth all that is needed is to raise the woman's level of consciousness to where she sees she has choices and is worthy of being treated with respect and kindness. She flounders because she never knew or forgot that she can say no, that she is just as entitled to a good life as anyone else. She made herself weak and a punching bag. She needs education to embolden her confidence and to extricate herself from unhealthy relationships. She has to decide to change her self-image. Otherwise, all the money, resources and help from others is wasted, and she returns to what she believes she deserves. It is not the job of others to protect her; she must take responsibility and learn how to protect herself.

Ask Better Questions

To gain clarity about what you need.

Anytime you ask life-destroying questions, you get a life-destroying answer.

"Why is he mad at me?"

"Why is he such a jerk?"

"Why doesn't he listen to me?"

"Why does he ignore me?"

"Why can't he understand me?"

These questions keep you stuck in anger, believing your husband is wrong, and you are a victim. Whereas changing the question to, "What could I do differently that would work for us both?" is a life-supporting question. You are now coming from the platform where the outcome is a win-win. There is no anger, no blame, no shame, no explanation, and no defensiveness. Asking life-supporting questions ensures that your journey finds solutions that benefit you and your husband.

List All Possible Options

To find the option which best serves you.

Writing is often more therapeutic than counseling. It's free, can be done almost anywhere, gives you time to calm down and usually elevates you to a life-supporting emotion. Ultimately you know better than anyone else what you need, so it's a matter of rising above anger and resentment to discover the ideas that will improve your marriage and your life.

Most everyone wants a happy marriage, however, what is happy? Each woman defines it differently. For some, it's having a husband who makes so much money that she doesn't have to work. For others, it's a husband who is secure enough to allow her to have girlfriends and pursue a career of her choice. For others, it's laughing and loving, regardless of how hard they have to work, or how poor they are. For others, it's how handsome her husband is and how good he is in bed. For some, it's as simple as he makes her feel like a queen and the most important person in his life.

Then there are those women who need or want all of these. Are they harder to please? Not really. If she is clear and consistent with herself and with others, she chooses only the men who might be compatible. If he is honest and not pretending to be what she wants

While still in an upset:

1. Describe the upset in as few words as possible (preferably less than fifty words).
2. Describe your reaction and/or mood in even fewer words.
3. List all possible actions you could do. Be angry, be outrageous, and be horrible. Simply free-associate and write down every thought that comes to mind as fast as you can. (My funniest action was, "Kick him in the shins!" Venting anger can be a release that allows you to calm down, and move past the anger, and to ask what actions might be life-supporting. The image of kicking my husband in the shins made me laugh; it was so absurd and never would happen in real life; so it amused me to even have it swirling around in my subconscious. Acknowledging this absurdity helped me to find better, healthier solutions.)
4. Keep writing until you get an ah-ha moment. This is when you have a thought you've never had before, and you know is brilliant, that doing this action would make you happy and would make your husband happy.

It is clear that the greater your challenge is, the greater is your opportunity to develop beyond your imagination into someone you admire. You have the chance to tap into your inner strength, that wellspring that lies deep within your soul, that is at the core of your true self. By not giving up, by believing you can be who you want to be, and can have the marriage you dream of, you will eventually succeed. Faith is stepping out into thin air held only by God.

Summary

You are now familiar with the scientific calibrations of emotions. By assessing your level of consciousness and the range you fluctuate within, you gained insight about yourself. You learned that while zigzagging up and down this scale is normal, that you have a choice to uplift yourself to higher levels. You learned that to decide whether or not to divorce that you need to employ these levels of higher consciousness, that you need courage, neutrality, willingness, acceptance, wisdom, love, joy, peace, and/or enlightenment. You learned how to elevate yourself up to these higher levels of consciousness. The exercises were as fast and easy as riding an elevator up to peace.

Congratulations on getting this far on your journey. You have taken huge steps toward your goal of deciding if divorcing is right for you. Take a moment to let sink in all you have learned. You did a clarity meditation which got you out of the fog of overwhelm. It increased your confidence, making it possible to navigate your way through this journey. You made a vision board, which made you take the time to choose what is most important to you, and how you want your future to look. You listed your victories, which reminded you of the many times you triumphed. Seeing those triumphs increased your confidence that you can, and will, triumph over this chapter of your life. You are stronger than you think, you just forgot how strong you are. Overwhelm and anger were the storms that stopped you from your inner strength. You learned to ask better questions, questions that promote growth, harmony and peace in your marriage and in your life.

Well done! I am proud of you. You have opened your mind, and embraced new ideas. New ideas led to changing you. It is beyond admirable that you are willing to change. It takes courage to change. Change is going outside your comfort zone; it's trying new things as an experiment. It means being willing to make mistakes, integrate what you learned, and keep moving forward. Changing you changes your marriage. Pat yourself on the back for focusing on positive change and raising your level of consciousness.

Serious spiritual change requires being ready, willing and able. It can happen after long and arduous study, or suddenly upon understanding yourself and your husband with newfound clarity. Your decision to commit to discovering whether leaving is right for you sets the tone of resolve which makes it safe for you to journey to find the answers you seek. The insights you gain from doing the processes in this book unveil what God wants you to do, what he has always wanted you to do, and which now you have the courage and willingness to implement. And thus, you are forever changed, for you surrender your upset to God and stop resisting being full of grace and compassion. Wisdom is knowing what you need. Courage is taking action.

Chapter 5

O = Overwhelm versus Opportunity

*R*eflecting on what you did, how you got to this point in your life, what you could have done differently, and what you want in the future, all raise your level of consciousness to courage. It takes courage to look at yourself. It takes courage to be honest. It takes courage to take responsibility for your actions.

Which means wherever you are is exactly where you need to be. How long it takes you to complete this journey depends on how willing you are to open your mind to new ideas and to learn new skills. This book guides you so that you can process through your journey faster and easier. Elevating your level of consciousness lifts you out of feeling overwhelmed. What had felt daunting and impossible, suddenly is viewed as interesting and challenging. Your situation no longer feels bleak and horrible, but is an opportunity to create a life that you like.

The way to heal yourself is not by berating your mistakes, not by punishing yourself when you fail, and not by blaming others, but rather to fill yourself with God's love and gentleness, to know that you are perfect just as you are, yet to acknowledge that you are evolving like a butterfly fresh and fragile from the chrysalis of despair and confusion, from the inward journey into your soul to understand yourself, and to fly with new wings and beauty into a blessed life that is your divine right.

Shame sabotages courage. Shame is the most destructive emotion, as it annihilates your right to be alive. It is far worse than guilt. Shame believes you are so bad you shouldn't exist. Guilt believes you did something bad. People hide shame as unspeakably disgusting, an evil that if known would cause banishment. Shame corrodes the fibers of your soul like cancer, silently eating away at your core.

Shame Is a Lie

To give up shaming yourself and your husband enables you to move quickly up to higher levels of consciousness, and life immediately gets better. You feel you belong, and thus have the right to life, liberty, and the pursuit of happiness.

Recognizing that depression is anger turned inward allows you to look at the anger you've suppressed, and to deal with the root of your depression. Change is always a choice that is always available, as though the universe holds its breath and hopes you choose a path which supports well-being, and empowers you to look at new options that work better for you and your husband.

Most people are highly intelligent creatures who thrive on change. In contrast, boredom makes you dull and fretful. Fear strangles you. Anger spins you in circles until you are so dizzy, you forget you have a choice and can get off that crazy-making roller coaster of blame and shame.

Divorce Was the First Time I Became Responsible for My Happiness

I remember the moment I realized that I could only please some of the people, some of the time. I saw how setting aside my needs was, in truth, not taking care of my daughters. Only to the extent I was kind and supportive of me, did I have the capacity to be kind and supportive of them. Being a single mom meant I was the head of the family. I no longer had a husband to take care of me; I had to be an adult all the time. I could no longer fall apart and rely on anyone else to take care of me.

Too often you blame others for your unhappiness. When you try to fit into your husband's or children's lives and interests, you risk becoming a shadow of them. You become a parasite, vicariously feeding off of their success and happiness. In the extreme, you shrink to near-invisible and feel unworthy of even having opinions. However, when tomorrow promises events that excite and nurture your mind and soul, you thrive. Empowered, you focus on bringing those dreams to fruition.

You think of God out there when in fact he lies within you. He is a part of every cell. You are a walking cathedral with legs that can move and lips that can talk. It is you who you need to apologize to for not honoring the miracle that you are. The ego feeds off of suffering. The ego chides and finds fault in everything you do. Is this God? How would it serve God for you to be less than he created you?

In every action and thought, you are in truth deciding to live in heaven or in hell. Not in the afterlife, but right now in your human life. It is the accumulation of each act or refusal to act that determines your level of consciousness and your spiritual destiny. Inaction is an action of not moving, not learning, not integrating, not believing in yourself, not having faith in God and refusing to honor the divine being that you are. Nothing in the universe is static. Even inanimate objects buzz with molecules moving so fast that they appear stationary. But they are doing what tables do, meaning that their molecules spin in such tight circles that to the human eye and touch, they look and feel solid.

What tight circles have you imprisoned yourself within? What ideas and beliefs are keeping you locked in an everlasting chrysalis, hardened with lies and shame, making it not possible to hatch into the glorious, graceful winged creature that God intended?

Shame is the lowest of all emotions. While it can be normal to fluctuate up and down this scale, soaring to joy and plummeting to shame, you resent whomever and whatever makes you sink so low that you would rather be dead.

Dr. Brené Brown, acclaimed psychologist and researcher of vulnerability and shame, succinctly summarized:

- "Shame drives two big tapes: you're never good enough, and if you can talk it out of that one, who do you think you are?
- "Jungian analysts call shame 'the swampland of the soul.'
- "Shame is an epidemic in our culture.
- "Ingredients to shame are secrecy, silence, and judgment.
- "Shame is not guilt. [Shame is] 'I am bad. I am a mistake.'
- "Guilt is 'I did something bad.' It is uncomfortable, but adaptive."

She claimed the antidote to shame is empathy. A person floundering in shame feels immediately better as soon as you say something as simple as, "Me, too." To acknowledge you have felt as low as them is to make them feel normal. They no longer feel alone or as inept. They lift from the quagmire of humiliation to higher states of consciousness.

A friend told me, "Perhaps you can never be happy because you can never have what was taken away." But I disagree. While there were many days I faked happiness to blend in and to avoid prying questions, it gave me time to mature and climb back up the ladder. I wouldn't be where

I am today without having gone through all those trials and errors. By making mistakes and integrating what I learned, I developed new skills. Each step was necessary and laid the groundwork for the next step.

The English alphabet has twenty-six letters. Without one of them, you could not create all the words in our dictionaries. Likewise, you need to develop the skills and maturity required to achieve your desired outcome.

Each time I arose from the ashes of despair, I felt stronger and had more feathers to fly.

Too many people shame themselves into not following their dreams. Shame keeps people from being their authentic self. From parents to teachers to religion, too often well-intentioned people clip the wings of dreamers. Repeatedly, you have been told not to be selfish, not to dream too big, and not to be idealistic. Bombarded with criticism, you doubt yourself. When you trust others more than yourself, you forfeit control, you forfeit center stage and settle for being a minor character in your life. You let others dictate what is important. Rationalizing that other people are smarter, more experienced, older, and must be respected, or that keeping the peace is more important than taking care of yourself, is to put yourself at the bottom of the totem pole.

Each time you let anyone cut your wings is like slicing off little pieces of yourself. Your integrity diminishes. After years of research and interviewing thousands of women, Dr. Brené Brown discovered the predominant motto of women was:

> *"Do it all, do it perfectly, and never show you sweat."*
> **– Dr. Brené Brown**

It takes courage to climb out of the abyss of self-condemnation. It takes daily fortitude to say no to others and yes to yourself. Yet, when you do, joy unfolds like a gate opening. Epiphanies seem to come out of nowhere, and solve problems. If joy prevailed in the world, there would be less discord, greed, mayhem, and wars. If joy prevailed there would be less sickness, less apathy, and less depression. When one person wins and everyone else loses, is it truly a win? Humanity needs to change its definition of winning to be life-supporting.

If you or your husband suffered from depression, that added another layer of stress to your marriage. Depressed people are hard to talk to, work with, and not any fun to be around. They are easily overwhelmed, easily irritated, and quick to flip into anger to defend themselves. Marriages need comic relief to ease tensions. Marriages need polishing to keep them shiny. Laughter rubs away grime, eases hurt feelings, and connects you and your husband in a special way. Inside jokes, that only the two of you know, make your relationship unique and dear to you both.

Depression is a global problem. According to the World Health Organization (WHO) as of February 2017 over 300 million people suffer depression and that number is on the rise.

"At its worst, depression can lead to suicide. Close to 800,000 people die due to suicide every year. Although there are known, effective treatments for depression fewer than half of those affected in the world (in many countries, fewer than ten percent) receive such treatments. Barriers to effective care include a lack of resources, lack of trained health-care providers, and social stigma associated with mental disorders."

– The World Health Organization[4]

Unfortunately, negativity is the pervasive theme on the planet as well as in marriages. Most people are quick to correct and criticize others. Few give words of praise or encouragement. The ratio is probably 100:1 or 1,000:1 of negative comments to positive comments.

Anger Attacks Blindly. Pride Gives a False Sense of Superiority.
DNA is programmed to look for danger. Before the time of newspapers and telephones, gossip was the only way to inform others that their neighbors, spouses, friends, or suitors were not to be trusted. Until the twenty-first century, it was more acceptable to hide behind ego.

Old habits resurface under stress. When tired, hurt, or scared, you resort to old habits. It takes courage to try something new. Yet, by adding more tools to your toolbox, you can select a better option. You can find easier ways to do things, and gentler ways to think. It takes wisdom to see that courage, willingness, and acceptance are your best friends. They are the friends that introduce you to joy. Wisdom is when you realize how negative thinking limits your ability to achieve the peace and harmony you desire for your marriage, life and home.

Vulnerability Is the New Brave

Today people are telling the truth in brand new ways. Where shame had kept people from divulging their secrets, they are stepping out of closets to expose their truth. From sexual preferences to being raped, from eating disorders to drinking too much, to being abused by a respected man in the community, people are finding support by banding together.

Cultures Are Becoming More Accepting of Divorce

The more accepting the culture is, the more that courage can blossom in a society, and the more people have a chance to heal and thrive. Western culture is on the cusp of an era where "be positive" is a buzzword and self-help books are bestsellers.

Joy used to be only a promise of the afterlife and only to those who merited it. Now joy is popping up in unexpected places like popcorn.

Kernels of hardened souls spontaneously combust with joy and expand into joyous creatures. Rags to riches stories are common; most everyone knows someone who got off of drugs or alcohol and turned around their life. Inspiring movies abound telling how a person or a team triumphed over uncountable setbacks and celebrated success.

Divorce is on the rise because there is much less the stigma of "a broken home." The divorce rate goes up in better economic times because the couple has enough money to live apart.

The Decision to Change

To choose the life you want and need.

The mind is stronger than the body. The mind can do an action one thousand times, long after the body tires, and can visualize each action done perfectly. Envisioning your marriage to be full of love and respect, playful and nurturing, and everything you want and need helps to manifest it to becoming true. However, several ingredients are necessary. First, clarity so precise that you can see it happening. Second, faith that it can and will happen as you see it. Third, the willingness to make it happen. Fourth, courage to make changes in yourself to spawn these new blossoms of joy in your marriage. Fifth, understanding that God meant for you to prosper and rejoice. Sixth, learning that until you take responsibility for every action, you are not genuinely invested in the success of your own life or marriage. Seventh, seeing that to squander the miracles God gives you each and every day is heresy as great as not believing in his mercy and power. Eighth, to not surrender your ego is to disobey God. Ninth, to fight with your husband is to choose war and make him your enemy when God intended him to be your helpmate and friend. Tenth, to let shame rob you of your divine inheritance of bliss and grace is to turn the joy of faith into a nightmare of discontent.

God's Song (sung in husky country style)

He stands by me while I am gone.
He cares for me while on the run.
In time and space I cannot hide.
It is to me that I have lied.
There is a hole inside of me.
He puts the sun inside of me.
And with that Son I feel so safe,
Because I feel His loving grace.
He brings me down when I fly high.
He does not like to see me cry.
But when I do, He lifts my mood
Tells me to eat nutritious food.
I need my God for He does see
The part of me I would not be.
He helps me so I will stay light.
He gives me strength to do what's right.
I need my God for He is strong.
He guides me when I do it wrong.
And when I stray, it's not okay.
I must become what He does say.
Obedience He wants of me!
Rebellion is no part of me!
The fight is gone, I never won!
But I am filled with His bright sun.
The joy inside, so warm, so kind.
How is it I could be so blind?
He opens up my eyes to see
The wonder of whom He calls me.
We are a team, a team of two,

He changes me to be not blue.
It is the time that we all see
We're not an I, we are a we.
The world is not as they do say
about to end and go away.
But we must work to live and play,
preparing us for a new day.
No longer can we all engage
in violence, and fear and rage.
We do what He did not demand.
Thou shalt not kill is His command.
[Written April 2010 after spending a month in Tibet]

Hence, if the goal is to save your marriage, or to divorce, not all paths lead there. Many a wealthy person late in life realized that it wasn't money or toys or bigger toys that brought them satisfaction. It was not until they volunteered that they began to experience joy. Too many people divorce and regret it later. Had they known then what they later learned, they could have saved their marriage, and avoided heartache, the disruption of their family, and ultimately had more contentment.

If you are mad or sad, you are resisting what is. Resisting reality is a fight you cannot win. You always come away bloodied and confused. It is not until you embrace reality, reframe it into what is positive about it, learn what it reveals about yourself that you are now courageous enough to face, and integrate those pearls of wisdom into changing your focus so that you support your marriage instead of burn it down. Think thunderstorm. Your tantrums are like lightening, and if hit home, ravage years of carefully building and maintaining your sacred haven. Discord rumbles like thunder. The nearer lightening strikes, the quicker and louder thunder booms. God meant marriage to be a safe harbor from the storms of life.

Realizing that change is normal raises your consciousness from fear to courage. Babies morph from single-cell organisms to growing limbs, brain, and heart without any conscious thought. Humans are programmed to change. Most of this change happens while asleep, and most happens so efficiently that it happens unconsciously and automatically.

Skin regenerates once a month. The average person loses 50 to 150 strands of hair each day. Blood is constantly renewing itself; some components such as white blood cells last only eighteen hours. Women and blood donors know firsthand that the body automatically replaces lost blood.

Change Is Normal, an Everyday Happening, and a Cycle of Life

It is only when you resist change that you have problems. The more set you are in your ways, the less willing you are to change. The less willing you are to change, the more shocked, surprised, hurt, confused, and overwhelmed you are by everyday happenings. Which means this journey will take longer and be more painful. Therefore, this book is designed to circumnavigate common pitfalls, so that you can easily avoid unnecessary conflict.

Why can't opinions be shed as easily as skin, hair, and blood? People who are thriving embrace change as a springboard to meeting new people, seeing and trying new things, and having brand new thoughts. You can view your situation as overwhelming or as an opportunity for creating a new chapter of your life.

If change is normal, why do people resist it?

When you come from courage and willingness, it is easier to drop your old ideas and habits, and show your true strong self. You can be flexible because you are not afraid of being vulnerable. You can accept change because you do not feel threatened. You trust you will survive and thrive.

However, fear, anger, and pride are easily reactivated and build an armor to protect the ego and prevent change. Those low levels of consciousness view change with suspicion and classify change as bad. This trio can be vehement because they are the ego's strongest defenders, and thereby the emotions which most fight against change.

To surrender fear, anger, and pride is a shift of such magnitude that life immediately feels lighter and better. It is the necessary leap to moving up the scale of consciousness into life-supporting emotions, and ultimately, getting to the end of your journey. Surrendering this trio makes room for courage to show up. It takes courage to save your marriage or to end it. Once courage takes hold, the willingness to try new things follows. These two friends introduce you to acceptance, which is a new perspective that mistakes are not bad, but useful feedback.

> *"The world of the ego is like a house of mirrors through which the ego wanders lost and confused as it chases the images in one mirror after another. Human life is characterized by endless trials and errors to escape the maze. At times, for many people (and possibly for most), the world of mirrors becomes a house of horrors that gets worse and worse. The only way out of the circuitous wanderings is through the pursuit of spiritual truth."*
> – **David R. Hawkins**, *Along the Path of Enlightenment*

Wisdom is realizing that shame, guilt, apathy, grief, fear, desire, anger, and pride are destructive emotions. It is realizing that in order to thrive you must embrace new emotions that support life and unshackle self-imposed limitations. You must move beyond the life-destroying emotions and embrace the life-empowering emotions of courage, willingness, and acceptance.

Every person has a dark side. The Chinese call this yin. It is the counterpart to yang. The two balance and complement each other. The Chinese have understood for five thousand years that every creature has yin and yang properties that naturally and inherently wax and wane. Yang is strongest at noon. Throughout the afternoon, yang diminishes, and yin grows until it takes over as night. Yin is strongest at midnight. As dawn approaches, yin diminishes, and yang increases until it lights the sky with the rising sun.

While you are born predominantly yin or yang, you retain some qualities from each. Both are essential, equally important, and neither are demonic. Yin is your quiet, contemplative side that needs rest, relaxation, gentleness, kindness, and listening. It is called "dark" as in hiding in the shadows, "weak" as in humble, timid, slow, and cautious. Yang is power and strength. It is light, energetic, bold, loud, and assertive.

Humans could not live on this Earth without the sun; likewise, no person can live without a fighting spirit. For life is hard. Life hurts. Humans have bodies that need constant maintenance. Lemon juice on paper cuts stings. Bullets kill. Harsh words shrivel confidence and take the color out of dreams.

Only the Brave Thrive

Most people settle for surviving. However, to thrive you must play the game of life offensively. By taking risks and making mistakes you learn, evolve, gain mastery, and ultimately succeed. And yes, you'll offend some people by not playing small, for daring to be different, and for daring to be you. Yet you cannot achieve your dreams by playing defensively because you spend all your time defending and explaining to people who cannot or will not change. Those people truly cannot see your vision. They never will. Don't waste your breath on them. It only wastes your time and annoys them.

In trying to open their minds to see what you see, what you're saying is that they're wrong. Human nature hates to be wrong. In the days of cavemen, wrong meant death. In the Middle Ages, wrong meant execution. Today wrong means shame.

The only difference between a hero and a fool is the outcome.

The hero rushes into battle waving a flag, the cavalry follows, and they win the war. In contrast, the fool rushes into battle waving a flag, the cavalry follows, and they lose the war. It is not by your actions that you are judged, but by their results.

Most thought Bill Gates a fool when he envisioned a computer in every home. Yet, today, some people have three computers. Not only did Gates achieve his dream, but others improved upon it. Computers used to be the size of a room, but today fit into your pocket, and are more powerful. The technology of cell phones is greater than existed at the time men landed on the moon. Meaning, it's okay to build upon the successes of others. Don't try to reinvent the wheel to save your marriage. Use this book as a mentor. Let it guide, teach, and assist you along your journey.

Know That You Are Not Alone

Divorce changes your life and all those around you. It creates upheaval in the best situations. It has a lifetime of consequences, especially if you have children. Or marry someone else with children. Blaming and shaming yourself or your husband is counterproductive. Only by working from courage and higher states of consciousness can you glean what is the right path for you.

The following chapters detail ways to elevate your emotions to ones that support life. Using these techniques will make divorcing easier. More importantly, these methods have reconciled estranged couples and turned their miserable marriages into playful and satisfying ones. To see beauty in all that exists is to see the flicker of joy in each person buried within their soul. This is the light of God, and the beacon by which he illuminates your divine path. This is his talisman of undying hope, always there, always available, to warm you when shivering, to embolden you when afraid, and to light the darkness when confused.

Summary

Change is a good thing. Think of nature. Hardwood trees drop their leaves and hibernate during the winter. In the spring, new foliage grows back thicker and usually healthier. The same is true for perennial plants which die above ground, but lie dormant, and grow back the next spring taller and wider. These are cycles of life.

You learned that your response to your situation depends on your level of consciousness. That you are reading this book means you are probably overwhelmed and looking for answers. Congratulations on believing in yourself enough to take action to improve the quality of your life. Understanding how shame undermines confidence enabled you to choose higher levels of emotions. Fear or desire led you to buy this book. Anger can be the rocket which blasted you out of self-pity and into courage. Recognizing that depression is being angry at yourself was a shock, but this epiphany catapulted you into taking responsibility. You learned that, in the words of Sandra and Daniel Biskind, "It is not until you step up to being one hundred percent accountable that you can make decisions which promote well-being."

> *"The human world represents a purgatorial-like range of opportunities and choices, from the grimmest to the exalted, from the criminality to nobility, from fear to courage, from despair to hope, and from greed to charity. Thus, if the purpose of the human experience is to evolve, then this world is perfect just as it is."*
> – **David R. Hawkins**, *Along the Path of Enlightenment*

Marriages have cycles of ups and downs. You know you cannot change a marriage by force; you've tried that. Demands, ultimatums, threats, complaining, fighting, pretending you don't hear him, ignoring him, withdrawing affection, refusing sex, haranguing, and being a pill don't work.

However, raising your level of consciousness changes everything. When you are in a higher level of consciousness people treat you with more respect. They listen more carefully. They give you more attention and more affection. When you get to the level of courage, your life begins to look like what you had expected. Courage is power. Ego is force. When relying on ego, every endeavor takes effort and does more harm than good. In contrast, courage relies on fortitude and integrity, the foundations of well-being. How can your marriage be whole when either you or your husband are shattered in fragments of discontent? God is like glue, but you pick the pieces. How do you know which pieces to keep and which to discard? Keep reading. The next chapter teaches how to understand your authentic self.

Congratulations on getting further along on your journey! You have leaped from overwhelm to seeing opportunities. This is like adding in all the colors of the rainbow, when before you only saw black and white. Take a moment to let all you have learned sink in. Pat yourself on the back for all the big, and little, changes you made in yourself to get this far. Acknowledge your newfound strength and courage, your increased moments of calm and clarity, and your increased understanding.

You are doing great!

Chapter 6

U = Understanding Your Authentic Self

$\mathcal{S}$ome people believe they are bad at their core, fundamentally flawed. They turned to God because he was the only one who loved them unconditionally. They rejoice in his forgiveness. They celebrate that he holds a place for them in heaven. Yet they cannot find peace because they cannot forgive themselves. They suffer in silence. God is the only one privy to their pain.

In this chapter you will learn how shame is the work of Satan. Shame robs your voice. Shame makes you lie. Shame makes you hide. Shame keeps you from doing the work God wants you to do. Each time you stray, he creates mishap. God demands obedience. Submissively following his demands requires giving up your ego. Ego is another name for evil.

Words are powerful, but not as potent as the energy behind them. Without changing intonation, the energetics behind the words are what the world feels. The same phrase can elicit affection or anger. Most people resonate from low levels of consciousness and are easily offended. Thus, confusion ensues. When communication is tough, your best option is to be your best self.

Reframing Nightmares

To gain wisdom from dreams.

A client came in upset about a dream she'd had the night before.

"My daughter asked me to take her one-year-old to Paris for the weekend, that she needed a break from mothering. That was strange because she's a great mom, always calm and cheerful, so I said, 'Of course.' Stranger that she wanted me to fly five thousand miles away, but she was agitated, so I didn't challenge her. In Paris, while changing the baby's diaper in a public place along with other moms, I went to the other room to get wipes, got distracted, and an hour later remembered the baby and hurried back. She was gone. Frantically, I searched everywhere, but couldn't find her nor could the policemen. It was the first time my daughter asked me to watch the baby overnight. Even if we found her, I knew she'd never trust me to babysit again. I woke up crying."

I explained the theory that all parts of a dream were parts of herself, and from that perspective to retell the nightmare, that she'd probably find great insight about what was percolating in her subconscious. She blinked and took a big breath digesting this new concept. However, it took her several minutes to let go of shame, guilt and grief to get enough courage to take ownership of what it revealed about her. The more she reframed the dream, the more her eyes opened wide.

"I got overwhelmed, and needed a break from mothering myself, that is, that newest part of me that's just one-years-old—guess that's the work you and I have been doing since my divorce was final—and wanted to get as far away as possible. I've always thought Paris a safe place, and romantic. But realized I wasn't prepared to be single again and needed some more skills, talking about going to get the baby wipes. How would baby wipes be some part of me? or the other moms?" She thought for a minute. "The other moms are the parts of me that are responsible, patient, attentive, cheerful, strong, brave, and capable. The baby wipes? I guess that's the wise part of me that cleans up my messes." She laughed. "Getting so distracted that I forgot the baby for an hour? And someone kidnapped her? Oh, well, yeah, I get distracted all the time. Yesterday, I didn't turn on the dryer because I needed my glasses to read the panel. We were at my parent's house, and the dryer was so high above my head that I couldn't see it. When I got to the living room to get my glasses, my dad started talking. He was so eager to tell me stories, that I sat down and listened. It wasn't until I walked back by the dryer that I remembered I hadn't turned it on! But how is being kidnapped part of me?"

She had to think awhile. It was like she had to search deep within her soul for an answer. A trickle of tears spilled down. "I'm embarrassed to tell you. I have a history of sabotaging myself, right at the moment of winning. It's like I see myself doing it, get excited, see myself celebrating, then poof! It vanishes. I'm always confused. It's like a dry orgasm; it started to peak, then fizzled out, no fireworks." She doubled over, her face in her hands, and sobbed. "I know the divorce was what I wanted, I know I'm better off without him, but I'm scared. I miss him. He wasn't all bad. What was I thinking? I didn't know it would be this hard. I hate being single. I hate going on dates. What if I never find someone? What if I never find someone, period?"

I let her cry for a minute, then agreed that there are no guarantees. "In each of your meditations, did you ever see yourself happy with your husband?"

"No," she whispered.

"What did the paths without him feel like?"

"Easy, fun, I saw myself smiling, twirling, dancing, and my house was filled with family and friends, and I loved my home, I loved my life."

"What about your kids? Did your kids show up in any of your meditations?"

She smiled. "Yes, we laughed and talked at dinnertime, which was wonderful because he'd yell or criticize the kids, and seems like most every night, one of them left the table crying."

"How are your dinners now?"

"Oh, they're great. The kids don't fight anymore. They help with the dishes. We turn up the music and have a dance contest. Who knew cleaning up could be fun?"

"So, back to your dream, does it still feel like a nightmare?"

"No, not at all. Viewing it that all parts are me, well, I feel it's trying to warn me, that I'm sabotaging myself again, doubting myself, when everyone agrees I'm better off without him. Actually, I don't care a hoot what others think, but I've prayed day and night, as you know, because I thought God didn't approve of divorce. You taught me how to calm down and hear my quiet voice, which I swear is God speaking directly to me. It's such a calm, kind voice, so full of love and clear direction. And it's never been wrong. But it's hard to obey sometimes."

"That's free will, but the universe holds its breath hoping you'll choose a path which nurtures you so that you can nurture others."

1. Whenever you have an unsettling dream, take ownership of each part.
2. This can be done immediately or hours or years later.
3. The more upsetting the dream, the clearer it is to remember.
4. If you have nightmares from childhood that still upset you, reframe those dreams.

5. Reframing downgrades a nightmare to an interesting dream. It's like quieting the wind of a hurricane; it no longer does any damage.

6. This process reframes nightmares so that you see the wisdom that they impart.

Journey inside Your Soul

To see how God sees you.

Shame is feeling that anytime anyone gets angry, it must be your fault. It's a life of always doing too much because you don't ever believe you're doing enough. Shame wants everyone to adore you because only then do you feel safe. It's hiding behind a facade of happiness to hide your misery. Very few know of the self-loathing, and the self-hatred. You'd like to be diagnosed crazy to be absolved of any wrongdoing.

Shame is being a victim, at the mercy and butt-end of everyone. Shame is the lowest on the totem pole of life. Shame makes you think you must relinquish self-respect in order to be allowed to live.

However, it is a choice.

Admittedly, it doesn't feel like a choice, but rather a yoke of banishment. But shame is a web of lies so old you don't know when they became your truth. It takes courage more than intelligence to believe yourself over others' opinions.

For me, it began with a resolve. I decided to go into the depths of my soul and tame the beast who lived within. It was time to see the real me. I was tired of running away to escape the horror of who I was. To conquer the beast or be slain by it; I no longer cared. I just wanted peace. Eyes closed, mind and body quieted, within a few breaths I walked down into an ancient labyrinth, into complete darkness. But this is meditation, make a torch appear!

Holding the torch out in front of me, I could see fifteen feet ahead. The walls were black, the hallway two feet wide, and the floor black and smooth. There were no smells, no sounds and no time. The ceiling was too high to see. I never looked back, that didn't scare me; it was what lay ahead that did. Not sure when I would meet the beast, not sure how frightening or mean the beast would be or if it would attack, I steadily moved forward, quivering. Part of me begged to flee. There was never a choice of paths, only endless ninety-degree turns.

Is the Soul One Big Labyrinth?

Probably only five minutes passed in real time, but it felt like a torturous hour. The narrow hallway opened into a small room with stone walls and an old, wooden table in the middle. Torches brightly lit the room. An old book like a Bible lay on the table. No longer afraid, I walked over to it. It had a weathered black cover, but no title. As I was reaching to open it, in walked my mother, grandparents and everyone I knew who had died. They filled the room. Everyone greeted me to celebrate that I had finally arrived. They gushed with love and joy. I was overwhelmed and delighted to see and hug them all. But I was puzzled.

Joy is at the center of my soul?

Did that mean there never was a beast? If that was true, how many other lies did I believe that undermined my health and happiness? How could I determine what was truth and what was fiction? At the moment I had the courage and willingness to meet my beast, shame evaporated like it had never existed.

Shame Is Illusory, However Real It May Feel

Someone truly cannot make you feel bad. They can only trigger the buttons where you condemn yourself. Of course, you don't like those people and avoid them, but they are not the ones at fault. You are. You are the one who gave their words the power to shame you. You are the one who believes you deserve to be vilified and exiled.

To go from shame to joy is not a fast zip line, but more like climbing up a rock wall with few handholds. The more faith you have, the sooner you have a safety harness. But it's still onerous work even for those with faith. There are lots of shattered hopes and silly slips, and lots of scares and exhaustion. However, the climb compels like the holy grail for joy is at the top of the mountain.

The ascent is arduous. It means holding on by your fingernails, and falling when they break. It means triumphing over fear of heights, only to get so tired to feel hopeless and slip, and then feel guilty for giving up. It means starting over, but this time stronger and wiser. By now you've learned that giving up wastes time, and you must conserve your energy.

With renewed gusto, you scramble up, but then are struck by a torrent of grief and an avalanche of frozen tears sends you careening down to the bottom. Shaken, surprised, disgusted, you rub the bruises and start again.

To Not be a Victim Is to be a Warrior

Resolve swells like hope, and anger fuels the desire to tame this mountain. Adrenaline and endorphins kick in; bloody knees and knuckles now look like earned badges, no longer something to whimper over. You climb swifter and smarter, remembering where the rocks were loose and which ones held your weight. You climb up with such ease that pride fills every cell and you scorn those who lag behind you, scoffing that they are weak and not trying hard enough. Eager to show off your strong muscles, you become reckless, arrogant, reach too far and career back down to the valley floor.

Shocked, humiliated, and wishing you could hide under a rock, you slump and sulk in a lump of self-pity. It can take hours, days, years, or lifetimes to rally and regain the resolve to try again. But joy is a flame that refuses to go out. It can be ignored and forgotten, but it flickers and waits, a day or an eternity, waiting to fuel your courage, and waiting to bring you peace.

After uncountable ascents and slips, and accepting you're not perfect, you reason that to not try is worse than failing. You begin to love that mountain; no longer is it an obstacle, but rather a barometer of how strong you are that day.

Rarely do your missteps make you fall to the valley floor, but when you do, you scramble up the mountain because those handholds and footholds are like a ladder. After thousands of ascents, the journey is in your long-term memory. It's part of your DNA to be passed onto your kids. Striving is thriving and leads to triumphing on the ashes of your shame.

Every time you refuse to be defeated by shame, you morph into someone stronger. You are born anew with more courage, more wisdom, and greater resolve. Life gets easier and joy becomes your new best friend.

The Courage to be Naked

To be authentic.

To reveal your shame is like being naked in front of the world. No amount of clothing can hide how exposed you feel. Telling others about your disgraceful or dishonorable deeds hurts like doing the deed all over again. It triggers painful memories.

To pursue your dreams is to reveal your inner self. To shine as your true self is so revealing that most people do not dare to show up as themselves in their lifetime. Usually pursuing your dreams means reaching beyond the boundaries of your current life. It means trying new things, having new experiences, and making countless mistakes. Your husband admonishes you to not strive so high because he doesn't think your dreams are possible, and he doesn't want you to get hurt, or to waste time and money. His advice is to change your attitude, and be grateful for what you have.

A person who does not settle for the status quo is deemed by some as restless or fickle, and can be accused of being impossible to make happy. Yet, frustration can be the grounds of creativity, and the beginning of exciting life adventures.

Likewise, a person who loves unconditionally is often viewed with a mixture of appreciation and suspicion. Some people cannot fathom such a big and undiscriminating heart, and feel uncomfortable around a person who is open-hearted, accepting, forgiving, and loves without restraint. To the extent you love is to the extent you open your heart. To the extent your heart is open and non-judgmental is to the extent you feel the pain that others are experiencing, and in extreme cases, feel their pain more acutely than they do.

Loving without shields or boundaries is emotional nakedness. It is so raw that it feels like there is no separation between you and everyone else, in fact, you can't tell where you stop and others start, that you are not an individual cell, but rather the ground matrix, the fluid like blood that connects people. This is a love so naked that it is palpable and on display for others to condemn or enjoy as is their choosing

Being naked is like being free. Whether it's giving up guilt and regret, or being physically naked, it is living with fewer encumbrances. To swim naked feels surprisingly wonderful. It makes no sense how removing a little strip of fabric can make such a big difference, but it does. Perhaps it is only psychological because nudity is not accepted in America, therefore, to be naked in public feels outrageous and a little bit rebellious. But the skin is your largest organ and to expose all of it is to feel more sensation.

You always have a choice. Regardless whether your predicament is due to your actions or the result of external happenings, you always have a moment when you decided how to react. Sometimes it was so fast that you missed the moment of deciding and flew into a rage, or stomped off indignant, or turned your back, or dissolved into tears.

Climbing to joy raises you above the upset so that the drama fades to irrelevancy. Epiphanies burble up, seemingly out of nowhere, offering brilliant solutions that make most everyone happy. Counter to what many people believe, joy is an achievable state, which can be learned. The more it is practiced, the easier and faster it is to attain. Even beginners can find joy within minutes.

It is hard to remember that you don't have to reminisce fights, nor resent your husband for his failings, nor worry about the next hellacious hullabaloo that has the neighbors wondering at what point do they call the cops. These are all options, but poor choices like drinking salt water; they burn when swallowed and dehydrate your marriage to death.

You forget that your mind changes channels as easily as a television. When feeling sorry for yourself, or mad at your husband, or overwhelmed not believing that any rainbow will ever shine amongst the black clouds of your marriage, take a big breath. Slow down long enough to inhale enough new air to clear your thoughts. When you get upset, you hold your breath. Thus, it is imperative to remind yourself to breathe.

To be authentic is to live with integrity. To live with integrity is to be of sound body, mind and soul. To be incorruptible. To be complete. This is such a high level of consciousness that you can count those you know who are at this level. Yet, it is attainable with diligence and by surrendering whatever else you value more than harmony, such as being right, proving your husband wrong, proving he let you down, and proving that you have been betrayed and mistreated.

To realize that there are other options such as joy and happiness is a leap of such magnitude that it seems impossible in this lifetime, so you endure until death brings relief and salvation. You don't doubt that God awaits you in the afterlife, and that he forgives your sins and transgressions. Yet, what would it be like if your ego absolved guilt, grief, shame, fear, anger, pride and vanity, and stopped nagging incessantly about each little and big mistake that you and your husband made? A seed is planted, the belief in a better marriage. A harmonious marriage is a better life. That seed needs spiritual nurturing, which when empowered by faith eventually synthesizes into experience.

Someone wise said the definition of insanity is doing the same thing and expecting different results. You are reading this book because you want a different outcome. These exercises can be done in any order and as often as you like.

Shame Exercise

To ease suffering and increase well-being.

1. Take a big breath.
2. Notice how big and easy it is, how much it fills your chest and abdomen.
3. Think of a time you felt shame.
4. If you can't think of a time, think of a time you felt guilt or grief.
5. Focus for ten seconds on this memory.
6. Notice how you feel.
7. Are you holding your breath? Does your chest hurt? Is your face pinched?
8. Now think of a truly happy time.
9. If you can't find one, imagine what joy might feel like.
10. Repeat the word "joy" twenty-five times, visualizing yourself having the best time of your life.
11. Has your breath expanded?
12. Have your shoulders relaxed and dropped down a bit?
13. Did a big inhale happen by itself?
14. Has the tightness in your face relaxed?

15. Does your mood feel lighter?
16. Does your body feel lighter?
17. Which is more fun and healing to focus on?
18. Which do you think is a life-supportive emotion?
19. Which would you recommend to your kids?
20. If you felt a difference, can you see how nothing changed except what you were thinking? The extent to which you are sensitive is the extent to which you have to be more vigilant of what you are thinking.

Your body reacts to whatever you are thinking.

Let's test everyday words. Your response can change depending on your mood, and there is no right or wrong answer, but this exercise demonstrates how words impact your mood. Most every word either expands or contracts your breath. It's easier to breathe when the chest expands, so you can improve your health and well-being by using words that relax you and encourage a bigger breath. Plus, you'll have fewer wrinkles, sleep better at night, and stop the hamster-wheel of negative thoughts.

Power of Words

To choose your words carefully.

The words you use have a direct and immediate impact on your body. Most people have a positive or negative reaction to most words, so it's important to find out your responses. Even simple words conjure up an emotion. The body literally does not know the difference between what is really happening and what your mind says is happening. Words, thoughts and actions hold such tremendous vibratory power that they sculpt your life. Gratitude is the key to opening new horizons, literally and spiritually. Complaint is a vacuum that sucks all that was good into a black hole from which no light can shine.

Words are powerful tools to be handled with care. Words can make or break a marriage. The mind is devious, easily manipulated by your ego, so beware. Your mind is a trickster, and finds sport in creating upheaval. The body is your vehicle; treat it well, fuel it with high levels of consciousness so that it can carry you to wherever you need to go to fulfill that which you came on the planet to do. Treat your body with respect as great or greater than you treat your car.

"The body is simple; the mind is complex."
– **David R. Hawkins**, *Along the Path of Enlightenment*

Thus, be careful of the words you use talking to others and more importantly, the wordsyou use talking to yourself. Most people have an ongoing dialogue inside their head narrating what is happening. Begin to notice yours. While listening to your husband, begin to listen to what you are saying to yourself. The following conversation between a client and her husband has their internal dialogue added which shows what is being thought, but not spoken out loud. This enables you to witness how and why they spin out of control.

"Hi honey, how was your day?" God he looks bad. Has he been drinking?

"Same as usual." Why does she nag me?

"Did you send out any resumes?" I bet he didn't.

"Yup, a few." Will she ever stop riding me about getting a job? I'm trying my best.

"Get any calls for an interview?" How long is this unemployment going to last? We need money!

"No." I'm outta here. I need a drink.

"Where are you going?" Don't you dare go out drinking.

"Out." Can't stay here. She's in a mood.

It's the internal dialogue that escalates tension. Relationships are always expanding or contracting, meaning you are either feeling good about your husband, or worried or annoyed about him. The greater the problems, the more they weigh you down. Negative emotions are heavy. Again, you can minimize their impact by minimizing what you tell yourself. It's not wrong to be judgmental, but negative judgments make you feel crappy.

"You'd never invite a thief into your home, so why would you allow thoughts that steal your joy to make themselves at home in your mind?"
– Anonymous

Emotions have an energy so tangible that you react to them physically even when no words were spoken. You know when someone is glad to see you. They light up, and in response you light up. You feel wanted and adored. In contrast, when someone shuns you, you feel rebuffed and often confused about what you did to warrant such disdain.

You maintain your garden better than your marriage. It's arrogant to think you don't need to pull the weeds, or fertilize it when you see fewer blossoms, or plant new seeds, or hoe, or turn the soil. Even good relationships need constant maintenance. The more you want your marriage to flourish, the more landscaping, pruning, planning, and research you need to do.

Resentment builds when people get lazy, or tired, or demanding, or overwhelmed, or bitter. It is said most relationships struggle with the small, petty stuff more than with big issues. That you're reading this book, you've probably tried all of the following, but if not, these are fun, fast ways to build rapport with your husband.

Building Rapport Exercises

To increase harmony in your marriage.

1. Date night: Once a week dress up like you did while courting, plan a special activity, and do something fun, that you both enjoy.

2. Spend a weekend without the kids: Hire a babysitter to watch the kids for one or two nights, so that you have undistracted time for just the two of you. Pick a sitter the kids adore, and they'll beg you to leave them alone again.

3. Alternate who picks: On your day off, do something together. Alternate each week who picks the activity. Try to pick things you both like, but also introduce each other to new things.

4. Do activities separately: While it is great to do things together, it is good to also do things separately. It introduces you to activities you would not otherwise try, and widens your social circle.

5. Decide to get mad later: Postpone your upset until later, after the kids are in bed, or after your husband goes to work, and enjoy the activity at hand. Often, you'll find you're not as upset later, meaning you lessened the upset in the moment, and in the future. Marvel that you can do this, that you are not at the whim of your ego, and that you can control your emotions. This demonstrates that you choose to be upset, and therefore, can just as easily choose not to be upset. Choose harmony.

"To win in life means to give up the obsession of 'who's at fault.' Graciousness is far more powerful than belligerence. It is better to succeed than to win."

– David R. Hawkins, *Power vs. Force*

When Communication Is Tough

To increase camaraderie with your husband.

When your husband isn't good about talking, sit close enough to take both his hands in yours, look him in the eye, and calmly speak to him. Make it as short as possible, and as positive as possible, starting and ending with what you appreciate about him, but be honest without accusing him. Start sentences with "I feel..." so that you take ownership.

Focus on the present. Rehashing past problems makes them today's problems.

Focus on what he can do that would be of help. Complaining only confuses him and raises his defenses. However, saying, "It would really help if you would throw out the trash when it is full," is specific. It is tangible, measurable, and accountable. Negative thoughts make specific muscles go weak, they rob you of confidence. However, replacing those thoughts with positive ideas makes the same muscles immediately strong. They create harmony instead of discord. Your husband begins to like and trust you. The more he likes you, the harder he works to please you. Men are little boys hungry for praise. Praise validates that they have been good and are safe.

Communication happens beyond using words. Many self-awareness classes do an exercise where you repeat one phrase, such as, "The eagles are coming." Your partner then tells you the emotion they felt. You confirm whether that was the emotion you were thinking. It's uncanny how often they are right, even though you speak in a monotone, void of inflection, and use your best poker face.

You don't have to use words for your husband to know that you're mad at him, disappointed with him, no longer in love with him, or considering leaving him. He feels it. He may not have yet put the feelings into words, but subconsciously, he feels the withdrawal of your affection and respect.

Therefore, raising your level of consciousness to neutrality, willingness, and acceptance has the power to turn your miserable marriage into a loving marriage. As said before, you cannot change your husband, and every effort that you try will build the wall between you higher, so your only hope is to raise your own energy level. From clarity comes perspective, from perspective come new choices, and from choice you decide what is best for you and your family.

Be Your Best Self

To bring harmony to your home.

When angry or heart-broken, and blaming your husband for your upset, look to see if you are upset at yourself. Take him out of the equation. What life-supporting actions did you take? If you're upset, you're wallowing in marriage-destroying emotions. You forgot that only courage, neutrality, willingness, acceptance, reason, love, joy, and peace are the magic carpets that can fly you to harmony.

Stop being dramatic. Stop thinking he has to change for you to be a better person. Stop thinking you have to make huge changes, like divorcing or moving out, to get the life you want. Instead, determine what small thing you need to take care of yourself. Often, it's less than you think. See your husband as your equal, lessen your expectations, and surrender upset to see the marvels which abound, the miracles in everyday living. The act of surrendering alone brings peace. Try it now. Repeat "surrender" five times. Notice how your face goes slack, your shoulders drop and your mind goes quiet. You are a junkie to tension. Every night immediately increase relaxation by repeating the word "surrender" a few times until sleep comes easily.

Taking responsibility for your life immediately builds confidence and inspires action. It puts you in the driver's seat. You are no longer the passenger being carried along at the whims of others. You suddenly have choice. You always did, but it's easy to fall victim and forget that not choosing is a choice, too.

To thrive means to be your best self. It is beyond safety and surviving. It is beyond enduring and enthusiasm. It is beyond adapting and accepting. It is higher on the consciousness scale than forgiving, respect, and courage. It's when you begin to shine with inner joy.

Some call this self-actualization, but that sounds too new age and indefinite, so I prefer to call it thriving. To thrive you must do what enlivens your soul, what excites the core of your body, what compels you and needs no validation, though you may not know why. It's like doing what God wants you to do, and not second-guessing him. It's being connected with all, and "in the flow." Joy rejuvenates the spirit, is the sunlight of the soul, and you were born with it. Every person in every country in every walk of life has a pilot light of joy below his or her bellybutton.

When you are happy, you tolerate disappointments and annoyances with grace. Keeping your energy level above two hundred, at courage or higher, you maintain equanimity. This feels impossible while drowning in life-destroying emotions, and it is, as there is no way to attain harmony from shame, guilt, apathy, grief, desire, fear, anger, or pride. To serve God is to refuse slumming in those black emotions, and to devote your body, mind, and soul to flying high with God, with grace, humility, and compassion.

You don't have to succeed, but you do have to try.

It is daunting to try new things. However, it is easier when you don't have to succeed; if trying is succeeding, then you cannot fail. You are more capable than you think. Succeeding at little things increases your confidence. Confidence makes you more willing to try increasingly difficult challenges, and makes you more patient because you believe in yourself.

Path of No Tears

To gain clarity and calm.

Sometimes it feels impossible to know what to do, such as when what brings you happiness causes your husband grief, resentment, and pain. This often happens in a divorce. The person who asked for the divorce is ready to move forward, but that's because they've been thinking about it for weeks, months, or years, and it's their choice. In contrast, when this request, or demand, is sprung upon the other person, sometimes without warning, the shock is like the sun exploded and plunged their world into darkness.

How do you know when you're on the right path?

If you are a person who cries easily, you can use tears as feedback. Your body wants you to be happy, and if you refuse to follow its directives, your body gives you red flags. If the thought of reconciling makes you sob, don't reconcile. On the other hand, if separating makes you sob, don't separate. If your husband wants a divorce, and that makes you sob, calm yourself with meditation, and then ask these questions: "Is his love selfish?" "Am I better off without him?" "Is divorcing him saving me a lot of grief in the future?" If you get a yes for each, from this perspective it's easier to accept the divorce, and forgive him. You might come to thank him for setting you free, for you have the opportunity to find a more compatible mate. If gangrene developed in your leg, and amputating your leg saved you from dying, you'd amputate. Divorce is an amputation, even if you wanted and needed it. You are half of what had been whole.

Anyone who has succeeded has failed many times. Babies fall hundreds of times before they learn to walk. No one tells them to stop trying. However, it can be hard to know if a change is right or wrong, or good or bad. Good for whom? Good in the short-term, or in years to come? The bigger the change, the more you vacillate and feel uncertain which path to choose. Change leaves behind friends and family, and sometimes estranges them. They liked your life the way it was. They aren't sure they'll like your new life. Or aren't sure you'll continue to like them, that you'll change, find new friends, and leave them behind. At a minimum, you are evolving in ways that they are not.

When change is right for you, you will feel some or all of these:

1. Curious, excited, interested
2. Your energy perks up
3. You like your future
4. You feel your world is expanding
5. Your thoughts and ideas come easily
6. You feel connected to the world
7. You like seeing yourself on this path
8. Physical symptoms, such as hives, vomiting, headaches, rash, and ulcers, abate

When change is wrong (or when you won't let yourself follow what is a right change for you):

1. You implode, your world shrinks to protect yourself from misery as though being attacked
2. You feel confused, angry, depressed
3. You feel lackluster and apathetic
4. You say things like:
   - "It doesn't matter."
   - "It probably wouldn't have worked out."
   - "I was being ridiculous."
   - "I was being selfish."
5. You rationalize not following your dream, saying it wasn't meant to be.

6. This is the quintessential difference. When change is good, you feel the life-supporting emotions, such as courage, willingness, acceptance, reason, love, and joy. When change is bad, you flounder in the life-destroying emotions, such as shame, guilt, grief, fear, anger, and pride.

It can be hard to articulate your reasons to make a bold change because you truly don't know why you feel compelled, or are too embarrassed to share your vision. Most people are not free-spirited enough to say, "It sounds fun." Or even more controversial, "I'm not happy. This would make me happy."

If you are willing to take new classes, meet new people, and want to improve the quality of your life, you are courageous. In fact, the degree to which others question you is to the degree taking risks is outside their comfort zone, nor what they would allow themselves.

Change is taking risks. It's learning new skills. It means being willing to make mistakes and try again. It means not settling for less than your dreams. Dreams are windows to your soul, to your life purpose. Most people hide their essence, and keep themselves small. They don't want center stage even in their lives.

Thriving is what seemed hard yesterday is easier today. Working on dreams means at moments feeling overwhelmed, confused, failing, and sometimes feeling hopeless. It can feel like you can't get there. Yet, like video games, life often shifts unexpectedly and what seemed impossible is now possible. I call these Eleventh-Hour wins.

The Work of Byron Katie
To gain clarity and calm.

"I discovered that when I believed my thoughts, I suffered, but that when I didn't believe them, I didn't suffer, and that this is

true for every human being. Freedom is as simple as that. I found that suffering is optional. I found a joy within me that has never disappeared, not for a single moment."

– Byron Katie

The four questions she teaches to ask of every upset are:

1. Is it true?
2. Can you absolutely know that it's true?
3. How do you react, what happens, when you believe that thought?
4. Who would you be without the thought? [5]

The next step of The Work, "the turnaround," is a way of experiencing the opposite of the believed thought. For example, the thought, "My husband should listen to me," can be turned around to, "I should listen to my husband," "I should listen to myself," and "My husband shouldn't listen to me." Then one finds specific examples of how each turnaround might be true.

Bucket List

To map your future.

Making a list of the things you want to do before you die enlivens your body, mind, and spirit. The future is a blank canvas. Envisioning places you want to visit and things you want to accomplish creates desire. Desire is way better than shame, grief, apathy, guilt, and fear.

1. List one hundred things you want to do in your lifetime.
2. Be outrageous, be silly.
3. List things that interest you, but seem impossible.

4. Think back to what you wanted to do/be/see when you were a kid.

5. List one thing that is so outrageous it stretches your mind.

6. Have so much fun with this list that it makes you giggle.

Summary

You discovered that your true self is pure joy, which is mind-blowing. At your core is God (or, if more comfortable, replace the word "God" with the word "joy"). You were born full of grace. Yet people shrouded you in soiled opinions until shame blinded you to the truth. You learned that sloughing off shame elevated your energy level. Life instantly felt better. You gained confidence. The shame exercise demonstrated how your body reacted to the words you speak.

You learned that words either expand or contract your breath, meaning it is imperative to use words that empower you. It is especially important that the words you tell yourself in the silent narrative in your head are words that expand your breath. Taking larger breaths means you have more oxygen in the body, think clearer, and are calmer.

You learned that shame is illusory and never true. To give up being a victim is to be welcomed into the Hall of Fame of warriors. You don't have to succeed, but you do have to try.

It takes courage to be your authentic self. You learned that the Path of No Tears gives immediate feedback if you are someone who cries easily. You learned several ways to determine when change is right for you. Making a bucket list stimulated your interest in your future, and outlined the person you want to become.

Congratulations! You have finished the first three elements of your journey. "Journeying Takes Guts" is not a metaphor, it's reality. To change yourself takes fortitude, courage and determination. In the chapter called "Overwhelm versus Opportunity," you learned how to reframe what had originally overwhelmed you to seeing the gem of opportunity. These opportunities were hidden from sight due to your blindness caused by being upset. These newly-opened paths resulted from raising your levels of consciousness; by calming down you gained clarity and wisdom. In the chapter called Understanding Your Authentic Self, you dug deep inside yourself to see the true you. Your confidence swelled to see that strength, courage, determination, perseverance, willingness and joy filled your core.

Every exercise validated that you are on the path God wants for you. God wants you to be capable, courageous, willing, and wise. It can be lonely with God as your only friend, so know that I walked down the road you are on, and I am with you in spirit, holding your hand.

Mankind is evolving into a new era of understanding. Because the overall level of consciousness on the planet shifted from life-destroying to life-supportive, a quantum leap occurred that allowed men and women to embrace a God of Love instead of praying to a god of vengeance, guilt and hate.

Chapter 7

R = Reinvent Yourself
into Someone You Admire

People have said divorce is worse than a husband dying. Death is permanent, meaning you can never live with him again; however, you do not separate assets. No stigma. No angst whether you made the wrong choice. Divorce means no longer being married. Pictures become painful reminders of a love gone sour. The ending of a marriage is a death where both parties remain alive. To the extent you want the divorce is to the degree you positively move forward. In contrast, the more you do not want the divorce, the more embittered you become. Dealing with a bitter ex makes divorcing exponentially more painful.

Divorce changes your identity. You are no longer a couple, but a single person again. Thus, you must reinvent yourself. You need new strengths and a new identity. In this chapter you learn many ways to sculpt a new you. By elevating your level of consciousness, the new you is someone you like and admire.

How you respond to emotions determines your outcome. This chapter teaches ways to deal with anger. Making affirmations a daily part of your life changes the words you use to ones that build confidence and clarity. Quantum leaps are a way to try out different paths, from the safety and comfort of your home. Having too many options is as bad as having none. The first is dizzy-making, meaning you cannot decide, and thus do not move forward. The latter is imprisonment.

The Seven Chakras meditation works for beginners and experienced meditators. It is a powerful way to feel connected to God, and be filled with knowledge, clarity, love, strength, and creativity.

Your quiet voice channels the brilliance of your soul. Its wisdom and clarity are so succinct that you know it's not coming from your haranguing voices, those low-life scum that squabble, fight, and no one wins. It is a voice without angst, and without past or future. It is a voice so full of enlightenment that you wonder if you are hearing God speak. However, this voice cannot be heard above the mayhem of daily life. Fear, anger, and pride clamor in that inner dialogue, that non-stop cacophony of arguments and belittling. You must become still in mind and body to hear your quiet voice.

Beware, your ego panics when it loses control, and opposes the advice of the quiet voice. The ego is self-serving, narcissistic, conniving, hedonistic, and opportunistic. It wants what it wants when it wants it. Like a spoiled child, it rants, whines, throws temper tantrums, begs, and demands. In a word, it is mean and shallow. In contrast, the quiet voice is neutral, a high energy level, and the only voice which is never wrong.

In this chapter, you will learn more exercises to increase your clarity and calm, which get you further along your journey. Learning how to use laughter for stopping panic attacks and uncontrollable crying is a valuable tool in your toolbox. Sitting less and exercising more are scientifically proven to benefit most every aspect of your life. Learning how to incorporate movement at work is an easy way to get exercise when you do not have the time or money to go to the gym. Exercise immediately increases oxygen, clarity, and calm.

Regardless of whether or not you asked for the divorce, it was done by choice, and you signed documents to agree to it. Plus, usually you have to continue to see your ex after splitting up which, at best, is awkward. If you have children, you have to coordinate holidays and vacations. You didn't get along in marriage, so why do you expect to get along after separating?

California courts mandate that couples attend a "Children in the Middle" workshop. They encourage making the rules similar in both households for bedtimes, hours watching television, allowances, et cetera. This sounds good, but is impractical. Once separated, both you and your husband do activities that were "not allowed" in the marriage because the other did not enjoy or approve of them, such as traveling or retraining for a new career that meant being gone for six months. Think of the Venn diagram. Most marriages survive by doing things of overlapping interest or tolerance. Once separated, you and your ex do what had been given up to make the marriage work. Thus, in most cases, your ex becomes a person you would never date.

New complications arise when your ex is bitter. My first ex hurt so badly that he wanted to hurt me. He called several times in an hour, until I broke down and cried. After years of this, I hung up whenever he called and stopped reading his emails, for I only made matters worse when I responded. He accused, I defended or tried to explain, and we parlayed in emotional sparring. However, my not being able to deal with his pain and anger caused years of strife. Several therapists said it caused him to project his anger for me onto our daughters. It took the birth of our granddaughter before we could spend five hours in the same room without tension, and our family began to heal.

No amount of pain justifies being mean. However, like an injured animal bites the rescuer, pain and anger drive some people to being mean. The calmer you are, the calmer they will be. Contain the upset by not making it bigger than it is.

My second divorce was so amicable that we didn't hire an attorney. We discussed, agreed, divided our joint assets, and remained friends. The divorce occurred during my first year in China. The Chinese rarely divorce because it shames the entire family, including parents, grandparents, et cetera. The shame is so great it is like having the letter D branded on their forehead. Since I was more outspoken than the average American, I talked to my eighth-grade students about how I still loved my husband, and would always love him, but that I was happier teaching in China, whereas he wanted to stay in Santa Barbara at a job he didn't like, and to continue remodeling our house. We had been remodeling for eight years. Considering we were doing most of the work ourselves, it was slow. That was not my complaint.

I was angry that we spent a half-million dollars and were only half done. More upsetting was that the more beautiful the house got, the fewer people he wanted to invite over. This made no sense. My world shrunk to him, me, my Jack Russell, and the house. Also, the cost of living in Santa Barbara was so high that I didn't see how we could afford to retire much less travel. I love to travel, thus teaching in China was an ideal job for me.

In our nine years together, we had tried counseling with different therapists. I'd taken workshops, retreats, classes and read self-help books. I felt I was shrinking, imploding into someone I didn't recognize. Teaching in China was my latest, greatest idea to fortify our marriage. I expected to go for nine months and return with our marriage stronger. I was so sure this would happen that I framed a hundred pictures and created a gallery in the staircase, blending our families. I finished painting tiles for under the rises and installed them.

Within a month of living in China, it felt like home and a mother to me. I was happier in my apartment (the size of a double garage) than in my magazine-beautiful house mountaintop home. I had the energy to work full-time, to socialize with friends, do Tai Chi with the grandmothers in the park at dawn, and walk a mile carrying groceries. I was full of delight and gratitude.

However, the happier I got, the angrier he got. They say anger is really fear, and maybe he was afraid I wouldn't come back. He had little interest in hearing about my adventure. He didn't feel any relief that I was regaining my old self, the woman he'd fallen in love with. Instead, he wanted me to know what his friends thought of my going to China, to validate his pain, and to prove I was wrong to have gone.

I felt like a wife who had gone rogue. I didn't like feeling this. If I couldn't be a good wife, maybe it was best to stop being his wife. I'd built a new life amongst people who wanted me; I felt useful, helpful, eager, courageous, energetic and worthwhile. I felt compelled to be in China. Whereas to not be in China made me depressed, confused, nauseous, and scared.

When my dog pooped on the carpet, he gave me twenty-four hours to find a new home for her, otherwise he would keep her outside day and night. She was old and sick. His kids had been a nightmare, and I had cleaned up their messes, so this ultimatum felt unfair. But still, I was sure we'd triumph and be okay, stronger than ever, that I could take care of him and heal our marriage.

When I flew back at Halloween for a week, each night I counted down the days until I would be back in China. China felt like home. China was my happy place. I yearned to be back where I felt I belonged, where life made sense, where I laughed and was someone I liked and respected.

When by mistake my husband forwarded an email to our doctor asking if I had a pituitary tumor, while the doctor said he didn't think so, it started me thinking. In a moment of lucid calm, I decided if I had two months to live or twenty years, I didn't want to fight anymore.

We had fought most every day about the kids, the house, money, remodeling, and our future. But saying, "I want a divorce" stopped all our fighting. He just said, "Okay, I understand." It made me realize that loving someone isn't enough, that you have to like them, and it's hard to like someone who doesn't like most of your ideas.

At the end of that year, I asked my six hundred students to write about what they liked about my class and what they had learned. Several students wrote, "You taught us how to love." To them I was warrior-strong to share the upheaval I was going through, to shed tears of sadness at ending my marriage, and to sell my beloved house that I'd tiled, bricked, painted every room, and spent one thousand hours varnishing the ceilings and fir woodwork.

My ex and I remained friends until he remarried, and then he turned bitter and mean. After several unjust accusations and untruths, I stopped interacting with him. However, I keep in contact with his kids. I explained, "I divorced your dad, but you'll always be my kids." They seemed to like me better after the divorce.

Either way, you have to be strong to stay married or to divorce.

Anger zaps energy and tightens muscles. Anger might initially feel energizing because it spikes adrenaline which makes you feel stronger and more focused. It also spikes dopamine, which is a feel-good chemical. Between feeing stronger and feeling good, anger can become addictive.

Yet contrary to what most believe, you choose your responses. In fact, your responses are the only thing you have control over. Jack Canfield, the highly acclaimed motivational speaker and co-author of the Chicken Soup for the Soul series, taught this equation in his classes:

E + R = O (Events + Responses = Outcome)

Understanding and implementing this awareness is often the first step of taking responsibility for your life. Regardless of your past—of what you had or didn't have—you always have a choice of how you respond. Triggers can be years old and thus are like a knee-jerk reaction. They are so automatic that you forget and do not see how you made a choice. Yet, if you go back and slowly review your thoughts, you will see the thought that triggered the anger. *Mind over Mood* by Dennis Greenberger and Christine A. Padesky is a great book demonstrating how by mastering your mind, you can change your mood.

Do all people get mad?

No, some people laugh and turn it into a joke. Others shrug and don't react at all. It depends on your level of consciousness. The higher your level, the more confident, more secure, less judgmental, and more easy-going you are.

In most cases, getting angry makes the situation worse. The other person often becomes defensive and even accusatory, such as, "You're making a big deal out of nothing" or "I shouldn't have said anything" or "I should just keep my mouth shut" and then implodes in sullen silence and refuses to talk to you. Anger is a substitute for courage. Anger puffs up big and loud, and like the wolf in Little Red Riding Hood, cannot destroy higher levels of consciousness. Bravery, acceptance, dedication, perseverance, gratitude and tolerance are exponentially more powerful attitudes than anger. They bridge healing, harmony and humility. Too often what you call reason is in fact justification.

Exercises to Do When Angry

To restore calm and equanimity.

- Forced Exhales
- Silent Scream

- Anal Sphincter Release
- Stop Tears in One Breath
- Breathing Exercises
- Ha-ha-ha-ha-ha-ha until you calm down.

Note that it is important to actually say ha-ha-ha-ha-ha-ha, for when upset for it is usually impossible to laugh. Anger is spinning out of control in an effort to regain control. However, saying these words, in your mind or out loud, is a subtle laugh and lightens your mood. It gets you focused on breathing and gets you focused on calming down.

Fun Tip: Instead of writing "LOL," write "hahaha." In your mind, you hear laughing which cheers you in a way that the other doesn't.

Repeat these exercises as often as necessary. The more anger is a habitual response, the more often you will have to do these exercises. It takes a person thirty days to learn a new habit, but you will feel better immediately when you consciously choose to calm down. Each time you gain control over anger, you learn a life skill, perhaps the most important skill of your life. For in anger you are apt to say and do things you regret forever.

Forced Exhales

To reduce tension and insomnia, and increase clear thinking, calm and confidence.

Great to do when angry or having trouble sleeping, at bedtime to sleep better, in the middle of the day when sleepy, but don't have time to nap, and first thing in the morning because energizes and enervates.

This is a Rolfing Movement exercise and can be done anywhere, including while driving, as long as you keep your eyes open. It can be done as many times as feels good and as often as you like. Forced exhales clear out the lungs and increase oxygen. Like the Heimlich maneuver, however, gentler and can be self-administered. A Heimlich maneuver works because there is a pocket of air that isn't released during normal breathing. It has to be forced out in a hard, quick squeeze by another person. This pocket can hold up to twenty-five percent volume of air and could be years old, since it's rarely exhaled.

When you are tired, you tend to round your shoulders. Gravity becomes a greater pull. Your head migrates forward, and your chest collapses. As a result, your breathing becomes shallower and you reduce your intake of oxygen. By squeezing out this pocket of air and refilling it with new air, you increase the oxygen levels in your body and immediately feel more energetic and more relaxed. Increasing oxygen relaxes the brain and quiets the mind. The more relaxed you are, the sounder you sleep, and the less time you spend counting sheep.

1. Sit, stand, or relax in bed.
2. Take a big breath and exhale making a small sound.
3. Continue to exhale by squeezing the abdomen (stomach) until no more breath escapes.
4. You will know there is no more breath when you can no longer make a sound.
5. Inhale.
6. Repeat two to three times.
7. These can be done silently during the night while sleeping next to someone.

Fun Tip: You take shallow breaths while sleeping, using approximately only thirty percent of lung capacity, and thus awaken sluggish and stiff. Doing forced exhales before getting out of bed oxygenates and energizes the body. You can do as many as feels good. Add gentle stretching. Forced exhales help you want to get up and start your day.

Silent Scream

To alleviate temporomandibular joint (TMJ) disorder, decrease body pain, release overall tension and increase clear thinking.

Great to do this Rolfing Movement exercise when angry, overwhelmed, having trouble sleeping, or exhausted and do not have time to nap.

There is no coincidence that there are expressions such as "I swallowed my words" and "I bit back my tongue." People clench their jaws to keep from saying what they are thinking, or to hold back emotion. The tension locks in the jaw and facial muscles. Each repressed, suppressed, denied expression constricts the muscles until they begin to hurt. That's your muscles talking to you, telling you they have gotten too tight.

When you scream or yell, adrenaline releases into the bloodstream, which lubricates the joints and enables the mouth to open wider. However, vocalization is not necessary. Hearing a scream in your head activates this release. By keeping it silent, you can do it almost anywhere, even lying next to your snoring partner. Screaming is a great way to release anger. Silent screaming doesn't scare anyone. It's a fast way to go from angry to laughing.

Standing position:

1. Stand with your feet hip-width apart.
2. Close your eyes.
3. Clench your hands into fists.
4. Take a huge breath.
5. Hear in your head your loudest scream or yell, stretching your mouth wide and exhaling into the scream.
6. Squeeze out every bit of breath by compressing downward onto your knees and leaning forward.
7. Squeeze even harder until no air comes out.

8. Inhale.
9. If light-headed, wait to do any more until your head clears.

Lying down:
1. Close your eyes.
2. Take a big breath.
3. Open your mouth wide and exhale, do your "loudest" silent scream.
4. Squeeze out every bit of air.
5. Allow a natural inhale.
6. If light-headed, wait to do more until your head clears.

Since lying down is less energetic, it is possible to do the exercise more than once.

Anal Sphincter Release

To eliminate tension, increase movement in all joints and increase awareness.

This Rolfing Movement exercise consciously opens a clenched anus, and thereby calms the body and mind. Do when angry or overwhelmed and want to relax.

Most people walk around with clenched anal sphincters, hence the phrase "anal-retentive." As a result, their bodies and muscles are stressed from constantly being tightened. Right now, squeeze your sphincter. (This feels similar to doing a Kegel.) Notice what else tightens, probably your back and belly. Relax. Do it again and see if you can feel tightening in your jaw; squeeze as tight as you can and notice if your teeth clenched.

For most people, it is impossible to be angry when your sphincter is relaxed. Thus, when upset, relax this sphincter before responding. By keeping the anal sphincter relaxed, energy flows through you, allowing increased awareness and vulnerability. This isn't just a metaphor. The anus is the end of the line from the sinuses down through the esophagus and intestines. If you eat but don't eliminate, you die. Energetically, if you absorb other people's thoughts, feelings, and emotions and don't let them pass through you, the tissues harden. Eventually, this results in pain and stiffness in your joints and muscles.

Tighten your sphincter as hard as you can. Notice if your feet pull up, giving them less contact with the floor. This is because your legs are pulled up into the torso as though everything hangs from the shoulders. Relax. Which was easier on your body?

1. Invite your anal sphincter to relax.
2. Relax it even more.
3. Relax it to the point of bearing down.
4. Notice other muscles softening, for example, your neck and shoulders.
5. Think of someone who makes you angry.
6. Check your anal sphincter: did it tighten?
7. If so, invite it to relax.
8. Think of that person again.
9. Repeat until you can do so without tightening the anal sphincter.
10. Several times a day, notice if your sphincter is tight. If so, consciously relax it.

Stop Tears in One Breath

To release overall tension, increase clear thinking, and stop the flow of hysterical or reactive tears.

Great to do when angry or overwhelmed.

Say out loud, "Ha-ha-ha-ha-ha-ha-ha-ha-ha-ha-ha-ha-ha…" Exhale until you have no more breath left, for the inhale will be bigger, meaning more oxygen gets to your brain. Oxygen calms the body. If you are upset, do several of these exhalations saying out loud, "Ha-ha-ha-ha-ha…" until you calm down.

Most people are shallow breathers, meaning they do not take big breaths. Consequently, much of the air in their lungs is old air void of oxygen. Worse than that, when you are upset, you usually hold your breath which increases your upset. Breathing is how the body acclimates to all situations. Thus, the deeper you breathe, the easier you will weather the storms of marriage and life.

Exhaling until you run out of breath forces all of the stale air out of the lungs, and allows for new air to enter. This often doubles the amount of oxygen circulating in your body. Thus, there is an instant benefit. You immediately feel stronger, calmer, and more clear-headed. You are now in a better position to handle your crisis.

Breathing Exercises

To increase calm and clarity.

You are either expanding or contracting. It is impossible to remain static for long. When upset or tired, your chest collapses, rounding your back to protect your soft belly. The more rounded your back, the heavier your head becomes because it is forward of the midline and is no longer supported by the spine. Humans are one of the rare creatures who make their bellies vulnerable to strangers.

The more rounded your back, the less oxygen you can inhale. With less oxygen, you cannot think as clearly or have as much energy. Less oxygen in your system makes you less capable, which subconsciously erodes your confidence.

Focusing on breathing balances equilibrium for it distracts you from spinning with negative thoughts. Life doesn't look so insurmountable. If you can survive, you are safe. If you can smile, you are happy. Breathing is your best friend. It is the lightning rod which grounds and discharges rampant emotion. It prevents your being short-circuited and damaged by debilitating thoughts and feelings. Throughout the day you need to remind yourself to breathe, because you hold your breath when upset.

1. Say "breathe" over and over slowly and feel your chest expand with each new breath.
2. Does your chest get bigger?
3. Repeat saying "breathe." Does your neck stretch out like a turtle coming out of its shell? (If so, the muscles are releasing in your neck and shoulders.)
4. Notice if your spine lengthens and straightens.
5. Notice if your brain begins to have clearer thoughts.
6. Notice if your hips begin to swell as breath fills your stomach.

Because you hold your breath when concentrating, upset, scared, trying to remember something, and listening intently, intermittently throughout the day remind yourself to breathe. Take some deep breaths or Forced Exhales whenever you get angry, frustrated, tired, bored, or absorbed in concentration. If you have to make a big decision, breathe into the question first to calm and relax yourself. This increases the oxygen level in your body which allows you to make the decision from a state of clarity and ease.

The following is a list of ways you may not have thought of which you can breathe into and find relief. This can be therapeutic when trying to calm your mind at bedtime. Do as many as feels good. You will probably fall asleep during this exercise. Any order is fine. Make up your own. Repeat those that bring a noticeable sense of relaxation.

- Breathe into the heartache of your loss.
- Breathe into your hopelessness.

- Breathe into your headache.
- Breathe into your loneliness.
- Breathe into your anger.
- Breathe into your leg cramp.
- Breathe into the stagnant parts of your brain.
- Breathe into the tightness of your soul.
- Breathe into your disappointment.
- Breathe into memories that come unbidden.
- Breathe into things changing for the better.
- Breathe into relaxation.
- Breathe into falling sleep.
- Breathe into now, this moment.

In each, feel your body swell as breath expands your lungs and creates new movement in both body and mind. Confusion, pain, fear, and fatigue dissipate. You began life with a breath, and breath remains your best tool for contending with the pain and hardship of life. Breath expands compressed tissue, and is the key to unlocking the body when it shuts down.

Cure Panic Attacks in One Breath

To eliminate scaring yourself.

You panic because you cannot get your breath. The longer you hold your breath, the more the panic escalates. In truth, if you were to pass out, your body would immediately resume breathing. It is the frightened mind that panics because you are forgetting to exhale. Therefore, whenever you feel a panic attack coming on, say out loud until you run out of breath: "Ha-ha-ha-ha-ha-ha-ha-ha-ha-ha-ha-ha…"

Can it be that simple?

Yes, panic attacks can be cured in one breath. Why does this work? Because by saying out loud "ha-ha-ha-ha-ha-ha-ha-ha," you are exhaling. The panic happens because your mind won't allow your body to exhale. It is stuck on inhaling. Your mind is literally preventing your body from breathing. The more you try to inhale and can't, the more your mind panics, for there is no room for more air. Your lungs are full of air, but that air has no oxygen. Exhaling removes the stale air and allows the body to inhale. This breaks the cycle and ends the panic. Replenished with oxygen-rich air, your mind calms down because now the emergency is over.

Panic attacks feel like you are going to die. Once breathing resumes, you have energy and the wherewithal to deal with the problem that scared you. And the problem does not seem as bad as dying, so you feel empowered and more confident, as well as more clear-headed due to taking such a deep breath. Additionally, you rescued yourself from what felt like a near-death experience, so you are your own hero. To see a video on my blog about curing panic attacks, visit http://joyisgenius. com/2019/04/15-cure-panic-attacks.

The decision to teach in China unwittingly ended one life and began another. It built a foundation to start anew, to reinvent myself, to begin a career in a country where they spoke a foreign language, and everything was new and different. However, I am sure that I would not have gone if God had told me everything he had in store for me, for so much of it was beyond my wildest dreams.

If God had forewarned me, I would have told God, "Sorry, you need a braver girl."

God knew to only tell me what I could handle hearing. Because I thought I was only going for nine months, and if I didn't like China, would allow myself to come back sooner, I had the courage to go. That alone took every ounce of my courage. I expected to heal and build a happier marriage. However, as each unexpected event happened, it was surmountable. I blossomed in unexpected ways, so each step or misstep made sense, and I continued to thrive.

I would not be where I am today without going through all those trials and errors. By making mistakes and integrating what I learned, I developed new skills. Each step was necessary and laid the groundwork for the next step. The hardship or ease of your own journey depend how quickly you gain clarity. Clarity happens at the speed you see truth. Truth is that which is left when the clouds of confusion disperse. Truth only reveals itself when you are willing to rise above pain, suffering, being a victim, and surrender your illusions that you live in a world of right and wrong, and good and bad.

Whenever you react with anger, immediately choose to consciously feel love and gratitude toward that person. Notice if your shoulders drop and your body relaxes. Notice if you take a big breath. Notice if you no longer feel the need to explain or defend. Does life immediately get easier? Notice if your anal sphincter releases. If it has not, consciously let it go. Notice how you no longer feel angry.

Reframing Mistakes

To increase harmony in the home.

Perfectionism is another name for pride.

Are you so vain that you must be faultless? Vanity comes from insecurity, from feeling you're not good enough the way you are. That anything less than perfect isn't good enough. That you risk losing respect and adoration. That you fear banishment. This sounds melodramatic, but all low-level emotions are melodramatic. Shame is wanting to kill yourself because you don't deserve to live. Guilt is regret so huge you must punish yourself. Apathy is to disconnect from life because it hurts too much. Grief is unstoppable crying. Fear is seeing danger in everything and to destroy without compunction. Desire is lusting for spurious wants. Anger is hate. Pride is rationalizing misdeeds and misfortunes.

It is not until you cross the bridge to emotions that support life that the melodrama fades. Courage is the willingness to try something new, willing to fail, willing to learn, and to try again. Neutrality is seeing that there is no right or wrong, nor any good or bad, but all are equally interesting and worthy. Willingness is courage without fear. Acceptance is where peace begins, and a smile pervades your mind, body and soul. Reason is wise. Love is unconditionally accepting everyone and everything at all times, and holding them safe, honored and respected as an equal. Joy is calm. Peace is bliss, seeing the perfection of the whole. Enlightenment is godlike.

Mistakes are like a good dream turning into a nightmare. What felt safe, fun and reasonable births a beast. Big or little, that beast has to be corralled and neutralized. Restitution is needed in body, mind and soul. Take a big breath and look at your mistake. Say, "I did that. It did not serve me." Feel calm quiet your judgment, fear and regret. Take a few cleansing breaths. Feel your mind grow a wee bit wiser, your body relax, and your soul to find peace.

If epiphanies pop up, cherish them. These are ways you could have gotten what you wanted without forfeiting your integrity. Acknowledge that those options were not seen due to you being in a low level of emotion: shame, guilt, apathy, grief, fear, desire, anger or pride. Acknowledge how it serves you best to stay above those life-destroying emotions. To live with courage, neutrality, willingness, acceptance, reason, love, joy, peace and enlightenment is to dwell in the promised land of life-supporting emotions. Acknowledge that your level of consciousness rises each time you take responsibility and become accountable for mistakes, regardless if yours or others.

The smile on your face means you have grown wiser and integrated this mistake. You have reframed that mistake into a lesson. Life is a series of lessons. Thus, be gentle with yourself when you realize your foolishness. Choose to grow wiser. Grow wings of courage to go forth a calmer, wiser person. Be the example for others to follow. Be the wife, mother, daughter and friend who nurtures and uplifts others to be their best self.

Calm is the finest balm for discord.

When you genuinely apologized for losing your temper, and employed only positive words of gratitude, and your husband makes no response, you have to let him stay upset. It is vital that you stay calm, and give him time to forgive you. He will process faster on his own. Anything more that you say only confuses him. Stay cheerful, positive, confident, and quiet. He'll appreciate that you forgave him (for his part in the spat) and will regain his pleasant demeanor faster if you leave him alone. That he didn't apologize, too, means he believes you were the one at fault, and that he was simply reacting to your abrupt words.

If you are high strung, your pendulum swings wider. This is hard on your husband. He cannot fathom why or how you get so mad, and your intensity frightens him. Likewise, your soaring high on the wings of excitement confuses him, too. Sometimes it amuses him, but sometimes your moods are so foreign that he distrusts you. In truth, panicking only exhausts and disgusts you. You hate yourself for being pushed into acting frantic. Once you find equilibrium, you shake your head in regret, reminded one more time that upsets only block clear thinking, and make impossible the possible.

It's like you harbor two people inside, as different as Dr. Jekyll and Mr. Hyde. Instead of beating yourself up, embrace that you are exactly who you are supposed to be. Surrender your fallibility to God. Reason that maybe God wants you to go down this path to learn something you're ready to learn. Let peace envelop you. Feel the perfection of what is. From that oasis of calm, God speaks. You hear your quiet voice tell you the solution to your crisis.

If you don't get the outcome you expected, keep calm. Making others wrong loses kinship with people you need and like. Whereas when you give up the importance of winning what you felt entitled to have, you gain their respect, and increase their willingness to help you succeed.

On the other hand, if your husband drinks heavily, and his moods swing wide, his dramatic apologies get harder to accept. His abuse and compensatory lavish gifts, or tearful guilt, get tedious because they are too extreme. You narrow your eyes in distrust, almost not caring, partly because he was out-of-line, and partly because you resent being flung around like a dog's chew toy.

There is no reasoning with crazy. Your best strategy is to let his mood pass. In the meantime, your resentments build until you run out of patience. Punishing him makes him lash out in retaliation. Like poking the bear, he roars to intimidate. He hurts, so he attacks you, like an injured animal too frightened to understand that you want to help him.

When he calms down, or apologizes, ask for restitution. Restitution is asking him to do something that helps you and restores your respect for him. He is ashamed of his behavior, he just doesn't know how to be self-contained. He envies your comparative calm. He wishes he could control his temper. For example, the next time he apologizes with gushing words or an inappropriate gift, you say, "Thank you, however, what I really need is a new washing machine" or "the screen fixed" or "my car washed" or "for you to watch the kids while I go shopping" or "for you to mow the lawn." It must be something that he can actually do, and might do if asked in this way. If he riles in anger, wait until his rant is over, then state your request again. If possible, return the inappropriate gift. Not to make him wrong, but to clearly and pointedly demonstrate what you need more than that gift. Don't be "nice" for you don't serve him. Part of a wife's job is to check her husband's behavior when it crosses the line of being inappropriate, mean, or crazy.

Affirmations

To empower you.

Affirmations are positive statements that you want to believe. Your thoughts are so powerful that they determine how you feel. Your body cannot discern between reality and fiction. Your body responds to thoughts as though they are real, meaning when you worry or reminisce about a traumatic memory, your body responds as though it is happening right now. Fright, flight, and fight hormones release into your nervous system. Which is why negative thinking and reminiscing past traumas are not good ideas. You are unnecessarily scaring and wearing yourself out, and exhausting your nervous system. Stop this self-sabotaging behavior and turn your life around. Instead, use the energy you wasted on hypothetical fears and anger to make positive changes. This shift is as big as harnessing sixteen wild horses, who kept bolting and breaking down fences, to work in unison and calmly pull the carriage that is you.

Reminiscing over past trauma tears off the scabs of old wounds and makes them bleed anew. It triggers fresh pain and turns a sunny day into gloom. Even when your present life is safe, enjoyable, and full of love, remembering painful memories sends you down the rabbit hole into despair. To consistently choose to stay within the emotions which support life is like wearing a life preserver, buoying you back to sanity and grace when swamped by a deluge of anger, overwhelm or pride.

This is another example of how susceptible you are to your thoughts. Your body responds as if you were living the trauma, when in fact the trauma happened years ago. While your mind flits between past and future, your body lives in the present. The body believes lies. So tell it good lies, ones that support life.

If your body responds to what you think, regardless of whether true or fantasy or memory, you can build a bridge over this sinkhole by making affirmations. While many people teach affirmations, Jack Canfield's method taught in his book, *The Success Principles*, is the best because it evokes a stronger involvement.

Affirmations Log

1. Make a list of 100 affirmations beginning with the words "I am…" It is believed that "I am" is the most powerful phrase in our Western culture.

2. Add a strong emotion such as determinedly, excitedly, lovingly, delightedly.

3. Add a verb ending in '-ing.'

4. Finish your affirmation.

5. For example: I am joyously celebrating that this book is bringing peace and harmony to families all around the world.

6. Keep a Daily Affirmation Log on your computer or in a journal. Add to it when you want to boost your spirits. Read the affirmations you like best every day. Add "or better" where appropriate. Sometimes an even better house, job, or outcome is possible.

7. Affirmations turn goals into reality, or so your body thinks and responds as if true. This hardwires your body both consciously and unconsciously to do what is needed to bring that affirmation into happening.

Make a habit of starting your day with affirmations. Before opening your eyes, spend a few minutes affirming what you most need. For example: "I am joyously celebrating that my marriage is healed. I am determinedly learning how to rise up to courage and how to take full responsibility for my thoughts and actions. I am lovingly caring for my husband and excitedly seeing his true self. I am delightedly living my life in the way God meant for me to live."

Never include the word "not" because your body does not recognize it. For example, if you say, "I am delightedly rejoicing that my husband and I didn't fight this week" the body hears: "I am delightedly rejoicing *that my husband and I fight* this week." This is another example of how important words are, both the words you say to yourself and to others.

Using "not" makes a person think of that action. For example, "Don't forget to put out the trash," irritates your husband because it indicates that you don't trust him to remember. In addition, his body hears 'Forget to put out the trash.' Instead say, "Please remember to put out the trash." Compare the energetics of those statements. The first nagged; the second requested.

Seven Chakras Meditation

To gain clarity and calm.

Pamala Oslie, the internationally renowned psychic and author of Life Colors: What the Colors in Your Aura Reveal, taught this meditation in her classes. If you do not like to meditate and feel distanced from others, or if struggle to be quiet and still, try this meditation. It eases tension and aches, and energizes when you need fortitude or clarity to make decisions.

Note: This meditation is exceedingly calming, thus recommended at bedtime. It is easy to fall asleep before finishing it. When you wake during the night, simply continue where you left off, or start over. This meditation is also a good way to start the day. Do it while still in bed. Set the alarm if you might fall back asleep and need to be somewhere. It energizes and empowers you with fortitude, strength, knowledge, clarity, ease, love, creativity, and connectedness. Use it to energize yourself throughout the day by doing a shorter, faster version when feeling lethargic, dull-witted, or depleted.

1. Find a quiet, comfortable place where you won't be interrupted.
2. Close your eyes and imagine a white light from way out coming in through the top of your head, filled with all the knowledge of the universe. Allow it to course through your body, filling every cell, places that have been dark, or maybe never seen light.
3. Imagine your forehead opening wide, allowing you to see past, present, or future, anything you need to take a look at.
4. Imagine your throat opening wide, allowing you to speak clearly, concisely and with ease.
5. Imagine a light from way out coming into your chest, filled with all the love, adoration, respect, and honor of the universe.
6. Imagine a white light coming into your solar plexus, just below the sternum, filled with all the power of the universe, filling every cell from the top of your head to your toes. Allow it to come in and move all around and then allow it to go out through your back with equal strength, so it comes in through the front, circles around and then goes out the back, with equal strength.
7. Imagine white light coming into your belly filled with all the creativity of the universe, swirling all around and going out through your back with equal strength.
8. Imagine a white light coming up from the earth into your pelvis filled with all the grounded-ness, rootedness, nurturing and belonging you would ever like to have.
9. Take a big breath and allow all that light to expand until it fills the room.

10. Take another big breath and invite that light to expand until it fills your city.

11. Take another big breath and invite all that light to expand until it fills your continent.

12. Take a huge breath and invite all that light to expand until it fills the planet.

13. Take another huge breath and invite all that light to expand until it fills the universe.

14. Now, if you're willing, imagine there is a path in front of you. Perhaps there is some question you've been wondering or some decision you need to make. Go down that path. You may see things, hear things, smell things, or only see colors. Or nothing may happen. There is no right or wrong. If you are willing, follow the path and see how you feel.

15. Come back and try a different path. It can be a different solution to the same question, or some other question you have been wondering. Follow that path for some time down the road.

16. Come back and, if you are willing, try another path. It can be another solution to that same problem or something else that you wanted to look at. Follow that path some time down the road.

17. Come back and try an even easier path, an easier solution to that same problem.

18. Come back and if you are willing, try an outrageous path, one that is within your reach if you would only allow it.

Shorter Version

Open the seven chakras, but do not go down any paths. However, be specific how you want the chakras to open. For example, in writing this book several times a day I asked (taking an inhale with each statement):

- Open my crown to receive all the knowledge of the universe so that I know what needs to be included in this book that will bring the most healing.
- Open my third eye so that I can see and know what stories to include in my book that will bring the most healing.
- Open my throat for the clarity to articulate concisely and with ease what I need to share that will bring the most healing.
- Open my heart chakra to feel all the love of the universe, to the love of those passed over, of mentors still alive, of all guiding spirits, and open myself to loving everyone in a way that shares my best self and will bring the most healing.
- Open my solar plexus to receive all the power of the universe, to have the strength to have the courage to be authentic and share what needs to be written that will bring the most healing.
- Open my belly to have the courage to be creative in a way that interests people who are ready for change, in a way which inspires and empowers them, and will bring the most healing.
- Open my root chakra to have my feet on the ground in a way that allows me to soar and share with others that which will bring the most healing.

Fun Tip: Modify this meditation to fit you. Needs change, so change the meditation to focus on what you need.

Usually, I only see color when I go down these paths, but that is informative enough, for if the path is dark, I infer it as a path I do not want to go down; whereas if the path is light and bright, it is a path worth following.

Time is a nebulous thing in meditation. It is hard to discern whether what looks close is going to happen in a few hours or a few years. While you may not be able to see the actual events, a glimpse of their energetics is useful. Do this meditation frequently. If done at bedtime, you will probably fall asleep before finishing, however, it is a glorious way to quiet the chatter of the mind. If you truly need an answer, do this meditation sitting up.

Quantum Leaps

To leap to a higher level of consciousness.

Thinking of what you could have or should have done differently keeps you awake at night. Wondering what your life would have been like if you made other choices undermines your confidence. "What if" questions pester like a circling mosquito.

My client wanted to do life perfectly and got upset when she fell short of her expectations. She did this quantum leap meditation to see what her life would have been like if she had followed her father's advice. She was surprised to find how shallow that version of herself was.

Her "perfect self" vacillated between anger and pride. She was proud of achieving most everything she tried, and blamed circumstances and others when she failed. She had little humility or grace. She had little compassion or wisdom. She was a warrior without a conscience.

After doing this meditation she appreciated her many missteps and misadventures. Those painful experiences led to an increase of depth and awareness; she integrated what she learned and matured to be wiser and calmer. What had seemed failures were the quintessential steps that paved the road to her becoming happily married.

1. In a quiet place with an open mind, close your eyes.
2. Get as calm and focused as possible.
3. Be sure you are willing to know the answer.

4. Ask the question: "What would my life be like if I had..."
   - If you do not see any images or get an answer:
     ◊ You might not be ready to know this truth.
     ◊ Or that possibility was never an option in any part of your psyche.
     ◊ Try asking your question in a different way.
   - You might get a one-word answer such as "miserable" or get dream-like details of seeing yourself living in that alternate reality.

"The individual is thus like a cork in the sea of consciousness—he does not know where he is, where he came from, or where he is going, and he does not know why. Man wanders about in this endless conundrum, asking the same questions century after century, and so he will continue, failing a quantum leap in consciousness. One mark of such a sudden expansion of context and understanding is an inner experience of relief, joy, and awe. All who have had such an experience feel afterwards that the universe has granted them a precious gift. Facts are accumulated by effort, but truth reveals itself effortlessly."

– David R. Hawkins, *Power vs. Force*

Your Quiet Voice

To hear the voice of God. Your voice without an ego.

There are many voices in your head, each with its own cadence and timbre. Blame, shame, regret, worry, angst, shy, and fear sound whiney and pitiful. Hatred sounds mean. Anger sounds brash and belligerent. Desire sounds lusty. Pride sounds boastful and arrogant.

"Humanity is an 'affliction' we're all burdened with. We don't remember asking to be born, and we subsequently inherited a mind so limited it is hardly capable of distinguishing what enhances life from what leads to death. The whole struggle of life is in transcending this myopia."
— **David R. Hawkins**, *Along the Path to Enlightenment*

From shame to pride, these emotions are false, destructive, and do not support life. They cause problems. Pride looks good, but is blinded by believing it is right, and boldly, unwittingly, tramples others. Seek the truth for it changes as you rise to higher levels of consciousness; it is folly to assume you already know it.

Pride feels better than anger. Anger feels better than fear, grief, apathy, guilt, and shame. However, you do not begin to thrive until courage. Courage requires faith and trust. It takes courage to follow your heart into a future that may not be easy, and is usually a path less followed. You begin with a dream and improvise as you go along. Your quiet voice is a valuable tool for knowing what to do when confused, overwhelmed, or too tired to think.

It can be hard to know which option to choose when bombarded with a variety of conflicting voices. However, there is one voice that is so quiet that it is rarely heard. Your quiet voice is always in the present tense. It is often a one-word directive, such as "up" or "eat" or "sleep." It is neither proud nor emotional. It never argues, justifies, explains, or gets mad if you don't follow it. Do you have the courage to live neither in the past nor in the future?

Other voices chatter, complain, groan, argue, and remind you about obligations and previous plans. Those destructive emotions ridicule, and make you feel bad if you don't follow their advice. In contrast, your quiet voice is like a nugget of wisdom. It simply gives the optimal suggestion for your well-being at that moment. It is always your choice whether to follow its advice or not. However, if your ego is the dictator of your life, following your quiet voice will take extraordinary strength, and faith as great as living on the crest of a wave. Your ego will fight to stay in control. In contrast, your quiet voice never makes you wrong. Your quiet voice is the epitome of your spontaneity.

It takes godlike courage to live without a plan, map, or forethought. You must be willing to have uncertainty be the norm. You have to give up expectations, judgment, and opinions. You have to be willing to accept that others will judge, criticize, and perhaps condemn your lifestyle for they neither understand nor can fathom why this might be an advantageous way to live.

Your mind will ridicule your quiet voice because your ego is threatened. But that voice is not your quiet voice because your quiet voice is always kind, calm, and respectful. Your quiet voice is near your solar plexus, the region between your chest and navel. Your quiet voice gives information on an as-needed-to-know basis so is always your optimal suggestion at any given moment, even though your ego or others challenge it.

"The main function of this energy center is to provide actual momentum to move forward and realize personal desires and intentions in the world. It plays a fundamental role in the development of personal power. It feeds one's direction in life and the actions taken in order to reach your goals."[6]

For confidence to grow, you must forge independence from the opinions of others. Personal power comes from taking responsibility and control of your life. It means asserting your opinions, not to make others wrong, but to navigate your choices and use self-discipline to follow the path that is right for you.

1. Find your quiet voice by getting as quiet mentally and emotionally as possible. From this calm state, empty your thoughts of all judgments, opinions, and expectations.
2. Begin with a willingness to get answers that might not be conventional or even easy to hear.
3. As your mind quiets, notice if your shoulders drop. Does your face go slack? Is it easier to focus inward when your eyes are closed? Try it both ways.
4. Ask: What should I do right now?
5. If you don't get an immediate answer, rephrase your question.
6. Resolve to listen and follow the directives of the quiet voice for five minutes.
7. Increase this time interval to longer.
8. Regardless if it has been hours, days, or months since you calmed enough to ask advice from your quiet voice, you can do so at any time and any place. Your quiet voice is always there and always available to guide you. Thriving takes the courage to leap into the unknown and to have the wherewithal to seize opportunities.

Not every day was fun or easy working in China. Some days I awakened missing family so much I wanted to crawl back in bed and cry. But knowing I would lose my job and hence my apartment, I got up. After showering, I felt better. Getting up and moving uplifted my spirits. Seeing Chinese grandmothers doing Tai Chi in the park before dawn, and grandfathers hanging birdcages in the trees (to let their pets enjoy the morning air) put a bounce into my step.

However, after my daughter visited that second year, I had four weeks of spring vacation alone with eight bags of chocolates she brought from my father (who wanted Chinese kids to taste our chocolate candy). Chocolate is one of my best friends. But consuming it for breakfast and lunch, and reading forty books in forty days made my body swell and go numb.

An extract from my journal demonstrates how my quiet voice counseled, but I didn't listen. Because it is such a quiet voice that doesn't push or rail or shame you into action, it is easily ignored. As a consequence, I spent three weeks in a Chinese hospital, but oddly enough, I found joy. The bulleted sentences are my quiet voice speaking.

"Life sucks. I can't do anything right. I shouldn't even waste my time trying."
- Are you sure?
- What if you're wrong?
- Would you rather prove yourself right or be wrong?

"I'm going back to sleep."
- Up.

"No point getting up."
- Up.

"I have to pee. Jeez, I can't get back to sleep. My dreams are more interesting than my life. Pathetic."
- Exercise.

"I'm not hungry. I could have one piece of chocolate. That tasted good, guess I'll eat another. Yum, I'll just have another. They're small. That tasted good, I'll eat one more. It's gone? No! I hate when I don't know I'm eating the last bite. That's so frustrating, grrrr. I'm just going to have just one more. Okay, one more. Okay, I'm eating the last one, this is it. Gosh, I'm not hungry, no point having breakfast. Wow, I feel better. I'm not depressed. Wow, I've been productive. I made the bed, answered emails, took a shower. I'm a little bit hungry. I'll just have one candy while I make lunch. Okay, two more. Boy, those taste good. Three more. I'm stuffed, no point eating lunch now. This probably isn't healthy. No, but beats being depressed. Haven't been outside all day.

I'll just read one more chapter. I've read 150 pages? It's dark outside? Chocolate? No! I have to eat something nutritious. I don't have any food to make dinner. Guess I'll go out to eat."

When most of my body went numb, I went to the hospital. They ran numerous tests and called in a specialist from Beijing. The best part of being numb was that it didn't hurt getting a spinal tap. But Chinese hospitals are run like youth hostels. Meaning they're cheap, you share the room with strangers who may only stay a few hours, and you can leave during the day. They never found anything wrong other than swelling around my spinal cord, yet I wasn't allowed to check out until I could feel a tuning fork on my hip.

The first day was the hardest. Being told I couldn't read or watch movies on a tablet, but had to lie perfectly still, I panicked. *Go insane or find joy?* Meditation became my best friend. After seven days, they wanted me to bathe at a public shower before another battery of tests. "Can I go home and shower?" The nurse said, "Of course." My routine for the remainder of my stay, another two weeks, was to go home every morning and have breakfast, check emails, talk to my daughters, shower, play with my kittens, eat lunch, meditate during my three-hour intravenous treatment, go to a friend's apartment nearby for dinner, and sleep at the hospital. The best part was finding a gazebo on the hospital grounds to do Qi Gong. Old people in flapping hospital gowns and pushing IV poles walked the garden paths, so my exercising in street clothes with a hospital band on my wrist did not seem strange. Most thought I was Chinese.

My point in sharing this story is to demonstrate that even when you make stupid mistakes and do dumb things like living on chocolate and reading non-stop for weeks without exercise (to not feel lonely and depressed) that sometimes this is the path you need to take you to the next level. Those three weeks were like being cloistered in a monastery because almost no one spoke English. Devoid of movies or books, I had to find peace. Joy became my best friend.

I later discovered that expanding joy in other people's bodies melted their tight muscles. This was a welcome change from using elbows and force which are a Rolfer's tools. Not only did they feel relaxed, they felt blissed out. As did I.

The Tapping Solution

To heal an ailment or inability.

Three months later, I was back at the same hospital for non-stop menstruating. An ultrasound showed a growth in my uterus. "You're pregnant," the doctor said. Before I could say not possible, she moved the doppler around and found four more tumors. A bevy of interns observed from the end of my gurney. Being a mom, I was used to my privates being on public display. But it was odd to have strangers peek through the curtain because word got out that a foreigner lay there. Privacy is not a priority in China.

The doctor mandated that I stop taking the hormone replacement pills. Thankfully, the biopsy came back negative. Returning a month later to see if the tumors had shrunk, the doctor was baffled. The tumors were gone. My Chinese wasn't good enough to explain that I had spent hours "tapping" them away. Introduced to this method by a friend who used this tapping technique and no longer required open heart surgery, I tapped for hours every day. It is possible that the tumors disintegrated due to having stopped taking the pills, but tapping became a new tool in my toolbox. I have heard of others who have used tapping with great results. For example, Jack Canfield helped an attendee to one of his retreats get over their fear of swimming in five minutes by using this method.

The technique is best taught demonstrated, so watch videos on YouTube. Dr. Roger Callahan was the founder; however, Nick Ortner is a more well-known practitioner. It's easy to learn and works well in many different situations. At a minimum, it brings calm and focus. It also works on calming down anger.

Get Up and Move

The body gets tired of sitting.

Yes, you read that right. Your body was designed to be a hunter or gatherer. You were never designed to sit for hours. People who sit at computers or watch hours of television have more aches and pains than construction workers.

When sitting for prolonged times, at a minimum get up for five minutes every hour. That gets your blood moving, which increases productivity and creativity. When your body is sluggish or uncomfortable, it's harder to think. When the feet or butt go numb, this is your body begging you to move.

20-8-2 Regime[7]

To restore health, vitality, flexibility and well-being.

Ever notice that after sitting five hours in a car, you have little energy when you arrive? All you want to do is sit, which is absurd because that's all you have been doing. The mind is lazy, and when you hold a position such as driving, it locks your muscles in that position so you don't have to think so hard. Thus, to take care of your body, keep moving in order to keep the muscles fluid and relaxed. Hard muscles are tight muscles. Stellar athletes have soft muscles at rest. They know the secret of relaxing because tight muscles cause fatigue. No wonder you are always tired when sitting.

A sitting position forces the spine to lock to keep you upright. Also, over years the shoulders tend to round forward and you become hunched. A rounded back is the result of muscles shortening in the chest. The head is forward of the torso. Pain is felt in the neck and back because both strain to hold this position. Heads are like bowling balls. The further forward your head, the more strain it is to hold it there.

In contrast, standing engages the leg muscles. However, static standing can cause low back pain, thus it is important to place one foot slightly in front of the other and to make small movements in the torso such as rocking. Shift the feet occasionally. Swivel the hips from side-to-side. Move the shoulders. All of this can be done while typing. This is especially recommended for people with neck pain, low back pain, and ADHD.

Get fit while working at a desk.

Procedure:

1. Twenty minutes = sit at desk
2. Eight minutes = stand at desk
3. Two minutes = walk around

If you have the idea that exercise means going to the gym or jogging or brisk walking, think again. Doing small, gentle exercises while at your desk activates and strengthens your body. If you want more aerobic action, step or jog in place while standing at your desk. When you aren't typing, such as when reading documents, you can do bigger movements, moving the arms, or alternately lifting them toward the ceiling or out to the side. You can even side bend. The point is to move randomly to keep the body fluid. Repetitive actions lead to tight muscles. Muscles have a memory. The more you do something, the more the brain wants to help by locking you in that position, so you don't have to think so hard. But locking into one position makes it harder to do other positions.

The better you feel, the clearer you think, and the more energy you have. Exercising at work means you can fit in exercise even with a busy schedule. Exercising gives many immediate health benefits meaning you will feel better the first day using this regime. Standing at desks has become so common that some companies buy tall desks for their employees. If your feet become numb from standing for a prolonged time, alternately lift your legs. Some people stand for hours because they find that works best for their body. If you're new to standing while working on the computer, start with the 20-8-2 regime.

A computer stand is fairly cheap, can be bought online, collapses so easily stored, and adjusts for most any height. The degree symbols on each edge make it easy to align. It's lightweight and portable so can easily be used at office, home, or outside. Ergonomics are so important these days that many companies will pay for the stand. What increases your comfort increases your productivity and decreases your need for time off due to pain and fatigue.

Most mobile phones have a timer on their clock feature. Put your phone out of reach so that you have to get up to turn off the alarm. Once up, it's easy to pull the stand forward and stand up. Feel free to stand for longer. Do it as long as is comfortable. However, do not lock the knees. Locking the knees locks the spine, tightens the neck, face, and shoulders, and eventually causes pain. By making small movements in your legs and torso, you ensure that your muscles stay relaxed. Relaxed muscles consume less energy, and you will leave work with enough energy to enjoy your evening.

Why Don't You Move?

Feeling pain is so common that you think it is normal.

You want to finish and don't want to interrupt the flow. You become so hyper-focused that you discount pain because you are used to feeling uncomfortable. If you work in an office, it can feel awkward to move every twenty minutes because no one else is getting up to move. You might be afraid your boss will complain you're taking too many breaks. Therefore, go to the bathroom mid-morning and mid-afternoon instead of before work or during lunch. Get up to get coffee or water.

However, as soon as your boss sees you're getting as much or more done each day, and you're smiling more and walk with a brisker step, they might decide to try this regime. You might set a new trend for your office.

Stop and walk for five minutes when driving long distances.

When you're driving long distances, stop and walk around every hour or so. This will mean a longer trip; however, you will arrive with more energy and in a better mood.

For Long Flights:

1. Walk to the bathroom every two to three hours to make the sitting less odious.
2. Moving increases circulation, which reduces the risk of blood clots.
3. Moving relaxes stiff muscles making it easier to fall asleep and be more comfortable.
4. Older people generally sit more. Yet the more they sit, the more sluggish, weak, and frail their bodies become. Do this regime while watching television and eliminate the need for a treadmill. No need to move furniture, invest in expensive equipment, nor dip into savings. Get fit while watching your favorite shows.

FUN FACT: The fitness of American astronauts declined while traveling in weightlessness and NASA had to design resistance exercises to keep them fit.

Summary

Marital problems turned your life upside down. Divorce is a permanent solution, but creates a myriad of unforeseen problems. You must reinvent yourself to turn your world right-side up. Understanding that your response to events is what determines your outcome is the foundation of rebuilding a new you. You learned that courage, neutrality, willingness, and perseverance are your best tools because anger too often causes divisiveness. You learned more ways to buoy yourself up into the higher, life-supporting emotions.

> *"Support the solution instead of attacking the supposed causes. Frustration results from exaggerating the importance of desires. The difficulty with a closed mind is that it is innately prideful. The downside of pride is arrogance and denial. These characteristics block growth."*
>
> – **David R. Hawkins**, *Along the Path to Enlightenment*

Forced Exhales demonstrated that expelling air in your lungs injected a high level of oxygen into your bloodstream which immediately cleared foggy thinking and calmed your body and mind. You learned that screaming releases adrenaline which lubricated joints and injects confidence because you feel stronger. Screaming silently meant you could do it anywhere and at most anytime. You learned that releasing your anal sphincter allowed your entire body to relax. You learned that repeating "hahahahaha" was the fastest way to calm the body and stop a torrent of tears. You learned how to stop a panic attack before it started.

Learning that the body cannot distinguish between reality and what your mind said was happening sounded crazy, but the exercises in this chapter proved that to be true. You saw the value of using affirmations to rebuild yourself in ways you want to grow and change your life.

Quantum leaps were a fast and easy way to test out different paths to see which were better for you. Because so much of the future is unknown, being able to get a read on their energetics was helpful. Ascertaining whether a path feels good or feels bad was useful information and saved you time and energy. The Seven Chakras Meditation taught you how to pull energy from the universe to gain knowledge, clarity, voice, love, power, creativity, and belonging.

Understanding that you have many voices in your head—most antagonistic and rebellious, immature and sabotaging—but that one voice is never wrong, but is so quiet that it gets drowned out by the other voices, was to learn how to calm down enough to hear your quiet voice. This voice is like a direct line to God. Always available, always helpful.

The Tapping Solution taught a way to calm down, and was easy to do most anywhere. Understanding how movement increased well-being, productivity, creativity, health, vitality, and calm encouraged better ways to contend with problems in your marriage and life than stewing in an upset. The 20-8-2 regime demonstrated a way to get fit while sitting at a desk, required no gym membership, and made work easier.

Wow, that was a lot of information to absorb!

Congratulations on coming this far!

You are doing great!

You are over halfway through your journey!

If some of this material seems beyond your ability, be gentle with yourself. It takes time to reinvent yourself. This is not an overnight process. It took some clients years to give up self-sabotaging habits. To change is a choice, but that doesn't mean it is easy. It takes courage, stamina, fortitude, willingness, acceptance and determination to rebuild your life the way you envision.

However, sometimes it's too hard to make this journey alone. If you feel overwhelmed and want help, please email me at KathrynMacIntyreJOY@gmail.com.

Chapter 8

N = New Skills to Make Your Journey Easier

Contemplating divorce or getting divorced is hard. The issues and repercussions are complicated. Most everyone has opinions, some have condemnation, and others have horror stories of their divorce or stories they heard. It can feel like you're wrong if you do and wrong if you don't. In a word, it can be overwhelming.

Confusion, worry, and pride are tiresome friends. They get you spinning in circles, create doubts, and undermine confidence. The downside of pride is shame. Your ego won't let you risk that which you don't think you can do well. Pride can't stand being wrong or looking bad. It talks you out of some of your iggest dreams. It makes you a difficult person to live with.

Proud people criticize others. The sad thing is that they believe they are teaching by pointing out your mistakes and get offended when rebuffed. Because they believe they are being helpful, there is no arguing with them for they truly cannot believe any opinion except their own. Their minds are so closed that they cannot tolerate much less enjoy philosophical conversations. The world is black and white. Right and wrong rule their life.

By now you know that while pride looks great; it is hollow and destructive. Pride smashes those it loves with the intent to squish you into the person it wants you to be. If you challenge a proud person, their anger attacks like a beast, a beast they are proud to house within them. There is no reasoning with crazy. No words can change their mind. Your only healthy response is from a life-supporting level of consciousness. Courage gives you the option to stop being around them. Neutrality makes their opinions no better and no worse than yours, just different and interesting. Willingness means that you no longer need them to agree with you much less validate your point of view.

Acceptance means you accept them as they are and no longer feel compelled to elevate them to a higher state. Reason means you understand their logic, understand how their opinions make sense to them, and most importantly how your opinions are beyond their understanding. Loving them unconditionally means you are beyond judgment, beyond good/bad and right/wrong, and cherish them for being them. That doesn't mean you like them, but it does mean that they neither disgust nor offend you, that your level of consciousness is far above theirs. When you come from a state of joy, your view is from the clouds looking down on planet earth. From that perspective, seeing the big picture, all is perfect.

Your husband does not determine whether you will be happy, frustrated or disappointed. You choose your attitude, if only subconsciously or unconsciously. You are the author of the book called your life. The sooner you surrender your opinions, the sooner peace will be a part of your home.

It took courage to buy this book. It took willingness to read this far. Thus, you are of a high level of consciousness that supports life. Understanding the difference between happiness and joy is like crossing that line between sabotaging yourself and showing up as the true you. Learning how to do a meditation that elevates you to joy is a fast way to gain perspective. Perspective is needed in all things big and small. Perspective gives you grace, patience, and clarity. Once you have clarity, you see miracles in everyday things. Seeing miracles is to acknowledge the wonder of who you are and how God sees you.

Understanding that there are five levels of reality expands your mind and makes you answer the question: Which level do you want to live your life? There are no right or wrong answers, but only interesting ones. If this is your first time exposed to this kind of knowledge, it takes courage, neutrality, and willingness to look at yourself in new ways. This chapter teaches many new skills to make your journey easier. All of the exercises restore calm. Calm increases clarity. Clarity is needed to determine which path to follow to reinvent yourself.

Happiness versus Joy

You can fake happiness, but you can't fake joy.

The two are similar, but their differences are important. Even the English language puts them into different categories. Happy is an adjective. Joy is a noun. Happiness is a lower level of consciousness; it depends on external happenings and therefore is vulnerable. It can be taken away because the source of the happiness is outside of your control.

Happiness comes from pride, from having done or received something valued. It generally includes excitement and is accompanied by a story. You like to share these stories of triumph, such as winning the lottery, falling in love, getting a promotion, admittance to your dream school, graduating, buying a house, and getting married, to name just a few. There is a prideful quality to happiness that makes it feel right. People often congratulate you.

We have the word "unhappiness," but we do not have a word for "unjoyfulness." Happiness brings pleasure, but joy brings contentment. Happiness is a celebration that some part of life is great. Joy, on the other hand, transcends right and wrong and has a quality that all of life is perfect. Joy transports you into a spiritual realm.

You can take away happiness, but you cannot take away joy. Joy is the sun behind the clouds, always there, always shining. It is you who turns your back on it in pride or shame. You simply must clear the obstacles that keep you from seeing or feeling it. Joy is not a state to be achieved; it is a human consciousness you were born with. However, it got buried beneath lies you adopted at an early age. Those lies kept you stuck in anger, doubt, fear, guilt, grief, and shame.

Life is full of strife, hardship, and turmoil. Depression is rampant. A prideful showing of happiness sometimes makes friends jealous or even spiteful enough to pop your bubble.

In contrast, joy is far up the ladder of consciousness. It brings you immediately into light and ease. Joy elevates you above the chaos of the destructive emotions of pride, anger, desire, fear, grief, apathy, guilt, and shame. Joy offers love and a safe harbor to grow and create. It is uplifting because it supports life.

> *"Joy does not simply happen to us.*
> *We have to choose joy and keep choosing it every day."*
> **– Henri J.M. Nouwen**

Joy is contagious. Rarely are you happy during hard times, yet it is possible to feel joy, to rise beyond circumstances and connect with the ethereal essence of joy. In times of tragedy and amidst sorrow, such as a divorce or the death of a loved one, it is still possible to find an oasis of joy. This only happens if you can find and focus on that wellspring of your inner self. Love and joy make loss bearable. Love and joy offer warmth during the long, cold hours of grief.

Others may only see and react to the lightning and thunder of tragedy. But if you know how to access joy, you have the maturity, grace, and wisdom to find serenity in accepting what to others is deemed unfathomable. You accept "what is" without the arrogance of judging it as right or wrong. You transcend grief and are able to laugh and celebrate. You may have no explanation for the tragedy, but you need none, ask for none, and do not expect an answer. You surrender drama and thus feel peace. You rise above the weak emotions of despair, regret, and misery and revel in the much stronger emotions of courage, willingness, love and ultimately joy.

"If you choose not to find joy in the snow, you will have less joy in your life, but the same amount of snow."[8]

Joy Meditation

To release overall tension, increase clear thinking and elevate consciousness.

Great to do when need clarity to make a decision and/or rest from slumming in low-level emotions. Most people forget or don't know that joy resides within them. Yet, it is always there. To activate it and make it grow bigger, follow these steps:

1. Imagine a little flame of joy like a pilot-light below your belly button growing bigger with each breath.
2. As you inhale, imagine the flame growing even bigger.
3. On the next inhale, allow the feeling of joy to expand your chest.

4. On the next inhale, allow the feeling of joy into your arms and fingers.

5. On the next inhale, allow the feeling of joy down into your legs and toes.

6. On the next inhale, allow the feeling of joy up into your neck and shoulders.

7. On the next inhale, allow the feeling of joy up into your head.

8. On the next inhale, allow the feeling of joy into cells that maybe never have felt joy.

9. On the next inhale, allow joy to expand to fill the room.

10. On the next inhale, allow joy to expand to fill your city.

11. On the next inhale, allow joy to expand to fill your state (or province).

12. On the next inhale, allow joy to expand to fill your continent.

13. On the next inhale, allow joy to expand to fill the entire planet.

14. On the next inhale, allow joy to expand to fill the entire universe.

15. If you have to make a difficult decision, ask joy to help you.

16. Or, from this peaceful expanded state, do other meditations of your choosing.

Seeing Miracles

To increase awareness and gratitude.

You think of miracles as big things like what saints do by making a blind man see or restoring hearing to a deaf person. However, babies are a miracle that happen every day. Your body is a miracle. Without conscious thought, you breathe, your heart pumps, and you digest food. Inventions are miracles. Getting a man to the moon was a miracle.

To heighten your awareness, take the time to see, acknowledge and feel the miracle of everything, from nature to a bed to a refrigerator. Appreciating everything you take for granted allows you to marvel at the wonder of being alive. Your point of view flips, from complaining about what's missing to feeling gratitude for being so lucky to have this wonderful thing in your life. All feelings of loneliness, of not belonging, of not being on the right path, or not having achieved enough, evaporate. In that haloed state, you know you are in the right place at the right time and feel sublimely grateful to be gifted with so much manna from heaven.

This planet is a miracle. It supports an abundance of life from animals to plants. The variety of colors, smells, vibrations, inventions, music, and tenacity are impressive. Joy is an exceedingly high level of consciousness for it resonates with calm and gratitude. There are so many emotional channels to pick from, the bleakest being shame. Why would it ever seem a good idea to switch onto the shame channel? That's like flogging yourself with the past. Instead, commune with a hardwood tree. Feel its energy pulsating throughout every limb. Feel its cycles. Feel how it is okay with dropping all its leaves, valiantly naked throughout freezing winter, and sprouts anew in the spring.

The tree never says, "I don't want to be a tree."

Likewise, see the miracle of your marriage and your spouse. Whether your divorce is not important. See the everyday miracles that surround you, and from that high viewpoint glean where your path leads.

The Five Levels of Consciousness in Manifesting

To gain clarity in making decisions.

According to Pamala Oslie, renowned psychic and author, you create your reality. The universe is an all-night diner and you can order anything you want, like filet mignon, yet you keep ordering hamburger—month after year.

In her class called The Nature of Personal Reality, she taught that there are five levels of consciousness to manifesting what you desire.

"Level 1 Consciousness: if you have the desire for ice cream, you have to go out and work hard for the money to buy the ice cream before you get to experience eating it.

"In Level 2 Consciousness: if you have the desire for ice cream, there is synchronicity. A friend stops by with ice cream saying that they were thinking of you and knew you liked ice cream."

In the third level, you want ice cream and you know there is none in the freezer, but you decide to go and look anyway. Lo and behold, there's ice cream. It's easy to assume someone else bought it, but what if you created it? Just with thought?

In the fourth level, you want ice cream and snap, there it is in your hand. Obviously, this is a very high level that almost no one has experienced.

In the fifth level, she believes, "You have the desire for ice cream, then you realize you and the ice cream are 'one'."

Imagine looking at your marriage without judgment, without upset or blame or shame. What does it feel like to remove right and wrong, and good and bad? To simplify your situation to two people who want different things?

In which level do you generally live?

In which level does your spouse live i?

In which level will you need to live in to achieve your biggest goals?

Adding Intention

To empower yourself.

The mind translates experiences into words, and those words dramatically affect how the body feels. In his book, *The Success Principles*, Jack Canfield brilliantly taught how adding intention to your actions makes you more conscious of what you want. When you are clear why you are doing something, the mind gets excited and more determined, and the body responds with more energy.

- "I do this with the intention to improve my relationship with my spouse."
- "I speak with the intention of being clear and kind."
- "I smile with the intention of healing my family."

You get so busy that you forget the purpose of your actions. What had begun as fun became work. Your mind flits like a bee collecting pollen, always busy, never staying in one place long. You need constant reminders because life gets in the way. Interruptions, boredom, tedium, problems, unexpected events, illness, and tragedy are a part of life.

Stating your intention is a reminder of what you want. It gets you back on track with your purpose. It affirms what result you want from doing this action. Bees only have to make honey. We have careers, marriages, kids, houses, pets, cars, et cetera. Getting your mind to focus on what you want transforms everyday things into stepping-stones that pave the path where you want to go.

Walking Backwards

To improve awareness, balance and posture.

Walking is good for you. But what about walking backwards? The Chinese have been doing for it for thousands of years as they believe it keeps their brains youthful. It is common to see older people walking backwards in a park and alongside streets. However, you can do it on a treadmill, up or down stairs or to avoid the paparazzi, as Taylor Swift did on a hike. Tour guides are proficient at it.

Today, walking backwards has gained popularity throughout the world. It is regarded as the new way to enhance workouts. It uses different muscles, is easier on the knees, and burns more calories. "Your balance increases. Your hearing increases. Your peripheral vision increases," said Badyna (pronounced Ba-Deena).[9]

The chest opens and the body lifts toward the sky, whereas usually you walk leaning forward. It isn't boring like normal walking, and while it takes vigilance, it is surprisingly more relaxing than walking forward. I loved it, but what would teenagers think of it? I assigned it as homework. Not all liked it, and some complained of feeling dizzy or running into others, but an overwhelming majority liked walking backwards very much.

1. Go to a track that has lines and few people using it.
2. Scan to see that no debris is in your way.
3. Walk slowly backward, glancing over your shoulder occasionally.
4. Use the lines as reference that you're staying within them.
5. Notice how your chest opens and is easier to breathe.

Skipping

To increase vitality.

Whereas jogging leans the body forward, skipping straightens and lifts the torso, opening the chest. It vigorously engages the arms. It feels childishly silly so makes you smile. Especially fun to do with another person. Ask a girlfriend to join you. Hold hands.

Skipping is so outrageously outside of your comfort zone that it immediately lifts you to courage. It takes so much energy that it is impossible to think, meaning you get time to rest your mind and soul. Skipping is a fast way to leap up to a high level of consciousness.

Skip until you start laughing.

Listen to an Audiobook

To sleep better.

When you can neither sleep nor calm yourself enough to meditate, listen to an audiobook with a soothing voice. This gives you something to focus on and relaxes the body. Laying still with eyes closed is as restorative as sleep as long as your mind is quiet. This is rest so deep that you can hear, but you cannot speak.

Scientists proved that you learn while you sleep, so pick an audio that teaches something you want to learn. Hawkins proved that just the act of reading (or listening to) his book called Power vs. Force raised people's level of consciousness.

You can listen to an audiobook at such a low volume that it acts as white noise. Sometimes the night is so quiet that a ticking clock, sirens, a truck going by, a dog barking, or your spouse snoring keep you awake. Listening to an audiobook focuses your mind on something positive and the other noises stop being a nuisance. I listened to *Power vs. Force* day and night for months while in China, often at a low volume like white noise because it calibrates at such a high level of consciousness.

Read a Novel

To fortify yourself.

Usually fiction novels have worse problems than yours. Seeing them triumph over their problems makes you feel that you can probably triumph over your problems. Plus, you just survived an hour or more of your life while reading which makes you realize you can get through your current hardship.

Smile at Twenty-Five People

To increase well-being.

Most people won't smile first, but most will smile back. Strangers are friends you haven't met yet, and smiling is the ice breaker to making friendly contact. Smiling makes you immediately feel better. Being smiled at makes you feel good. Making eye contact connects you with another which enlarges your world. Most people look down while walking, too busy to notice much less interact with others. The more connected you feel with your surroundings, the safer you feel, the more important you feel, and the happier you are.

An elderly woman stood by her living room window each afternoon as the high school let out. She smiled and waved, and teenagers smiled and waved back. She did this for years. When she died, the teens said it made their day to see her smile and wave at them every day. They felt loved.

Hug Twenty People per Day

To increase well-being.

Hugging has been scientifically proven to increase well-being. People who feel connected feel less alone, less afraid, more confident and are more likely to smile. Hugging strangers is out of most people's comfort zone. Thus, doing so enervates you because it's unfamiliar. Yet, what is a little bit scary turns quickly to feeling energized. Apprehension turns into exhilaration. Doing something a little bit scary is like watching yourself become brave. Hugging validates that you are worthy. It means you are no longer invisible. In addition to making you feel better, the other person feels better, too. Thus, your bravery enlivens the both of you.

"A man with outward courage dares to die; a man with inner courage dares to live."

– Lao Tzu

Hour of Power

To energize your mornings.

Begin each day with

- Twenty minutes of reading
- Twenty minutes of exercising
- Twenty minutes of meditating
- Any order is okay
- Do these before coffee, chores, et cetera

This method is from Jack Canfield's book, *The Success Principles*. He said the sequence does not matter and that he mixes them up. I liked staying in my bed, warm under the covers, and reading something inspirational first. It unclogged the sleepy-dirt from my brain and got me thinking new thoughts. I kept the book and my glasses on my nightstand so only had to reach out an arm meaning I didn't have to get out of bed.

Set the alarm on your phone for twenty minutes.

Stiff from sleeping, twenty minutes of exercising is a great way to loosen up. These can be done as gentle stretching while lying in bed or more aerobic. Do what works best for you.

I found doing twenty minutes of affirmations was the most powerful meditation. Twenty minutes gave enough time to detail how each of these affirmations would feel when they came true. Repeating affirmations beginning with "I am joyously celebrating…" enlivened me to where I no longer needed coffee to wake up.

Mornings are a busy time especially if you work or have pets or kids. Yet, this hour is so powerfully energizing and puts you in a state that epiphanies often happen which makes your day more efficient and easier. Having nurtured your body, mind, and soul, you start the day at full speed. It's worth getting up a little earlier. However, I have known of people who shorten this to a fifteen-minute routine, doing five minutes each and get good results.

Sternum Lift

To improve posture and well-being.

This Rolfing Movement exercise is best done when you're tired and gravity seems a stronger than usual force. Your shoulders round, your head sags, and living is more of an effort. Add to that the hours of typing on computers and/or holding a steering wheel and over time, your back rounds and your chest collapses.

Without awareness, you tighten your bodies in preparation to fight or dodge. When you're tired or nervous, you round further in a subconscious protection of your belly. To the extent the head migrated forward is to the degree it became heavier. When the head sits on top of the shoulders, it becomes weightless, for it balances on the apex. Most people straighten their shoulders by tightening their back. This locks the shoulder blades which diminishes the mobility of the arms and neck.

Often, when the back hurts it is because the head is forward of the mid-line. The primary shortness is in the chest, but oddly the pain is in the back. To resolve the issue, you have to address the primary shortness. The sternum is the vertical bone between your front ribs. Inviting it to lift allows the chest cavity to expand. An expanded chest has a greater capacity to fill with air, thereby allowing a greater intake of oxygen. When the chest collapses, it no longer supports the head and the head migrates forward. By lifting the sternum, the base beneath the head is restored.

From a standing position:

1. Round forward and let your head hang.
2. Without tightening your back, lift the head.
3. Straighten your shoulders and notice the back tightening.
4. Move your head and arms around and notice their range of motion.
5. Now, round forward again and let your head and arms hang.

6. Invite the front of the chest to expand as if someone were pulling the bottom of the ribs outward.
7. Notice how the head comes up without having to engage any back muscles.
8. Move your head and arms around and assess their range of motion.

Arm Drops

To ease tension.

Tension in the neck and shoulders is not only common, it can be the cause of pain and numbness down the arms and into the hands. Sometimes, what is diagnosed as carpal tunnel syndrome is referred pain from tightness in the neck and thoracic inlet. This Rolfing Movement exercise loosens the shoulder girdle and facilitates more movement in the neck.

1. Lie on your back (knees bent or straight).
2. Arms alongside your body.
3. Close eyes.
4. Allow one arm to float up toward the ceiling, as though a string is attached to your wrist.
5. Keeping that position, invite a big breath up into that shoulder and on the exhale, allow everything but the arm to relax, allowing the arm to sink into the socket.
6. Slowly rotate the arm in small circles, noticing where it's smooth and where it catches.
7. Invite a big breath into that shoulder and gently move your head around to release the neck.
8. Slowly rotate the arm in the opposite direction.
9. Invite another big breath into that shoulder and sink further into the socket.

10. Allow the arm to drop alongside your body, letting go from the shoulder so that the arm drops as a whole.

11. Repeat that same arm, inviting more breath into the shoulder.

12. Allow the arm to drop from the shoulder as if there was no need to protect it, allowing it to plop alongside your body, keeping the elbow rigid so that the release happens from the shoulder.

13. Repeat the same arm, each time leading with the wrist and allowing the arm to float up effortlessly.

14. Do the other arm and repeat the procedure.

Faster Version:

1. If you're pressed for time or too tired to do this procedure, you can lift both arms simultaneously.

2. Inhale deeply into both shoulders and allow both arms to drop at the same time.

3. Repeat three times.

4. During each inhale, invite the chest to expand further.

5. Each time you drop the arms, let them fall with less resistance.

Spinal Release

To decrease tension and increase clear thinking.

You were never designed to sit; you were designed to squat. While squatting, the legs support the body and enable the spine to move freely. Sitting, on the other hand, disengages the legs, tilts the pelvis backward and forces us to lock the back to gain stability. This C-curve collapses the sternum and decreases the volume of the breath, thereby reducing the amount of oxygen intake. Over time, the shoulders round and inch up toward the ears, the head migrates forward, it gets harder to stand up straight and it gets harder to think.

This exercise from Rolfing Movement can be done for as little as five minutes or up to two hours. When it stops feeling good, get up. You can do this exercise by simply lying in the position and resting to the point of napping, or, if you prefer to be more proactive, experiment with the suggested movements.

Faster Version:

1. Lie on your back on a carpeted surface.
2. Position your legs over a couch, ottoman, chair, or bed; whatever will allow your thighs to be ninety degrees to your body and your calves ninety degrees to your legs.
3. Rest arms comfortably alongside your body.

Longer Process:

1. Lie on your back on a carpeted surface.
2. Position your legs over a couch, ottoman, chair, or bed; whatever will allow your thighs to be ninety degrees to your body and your calves ninety degrees to your legs.
3. Rest arms comfortably alongside your body.
4. Inhale deeply by inviting the breath to the top of your head.
5. While exhaling, invite your body to melt into the floor, letting go of any muscles which engaged on the inhale.
6. Without awareness, people often tighten their face, neck, feet, and/or legs as part of a big breath, so, if you did, invite those muscles to relax.
7. Repeat, each time melting even more.
8. As though the spine is growing long, tuck your tailbone gently and hold it in this position while inhaling deeply.
9. Release on the exhale and let go of all muscles which contracted to make that motion.
10. Tuck again with a big breath.
11. Release on the exhale.

12. Tuck downwards as though the front of the spine is growing long and invite a big breath.

13. Relax on the exhale.

14. Tuck upwards again and take a big breath.

15. Release and relax on exhale.

16. Invite a big breath into one shoulder.

17. Exhale and melt even more into the floor.

18. Invite a big breath into the other shoulder and compare it to the first shoulder: Was it harder to breathe into? Did less air fill the tissue? If so, invite a few breaths into that shoulder to expand it further.

19. Alternate breaths into the shoulders until they seem similar.

20. You can continue movement in any direction. Comparison is a great way to assess differences, and when you find a restricted area, invite breath and movement into it until it moves with greater ease.

Bringing the Foreground to You

To increase ease, calm and confidence.

When you walk, you are usually intent about getting somewhere. The more intent you are, the more your body leans forward. Anytime your body leans forward, it puts strain on the neck and back. An alternative method is to allow the foreground to come to you. You still move forward, however, you give up the effort "to get somewhere." What would it be like to glide instead of stride? To have your shoulders center over your hips instead of being forward of the mid-line? To have your head centered on your shoulders instead of reaching out like a turtle? It might be a lot more comfortable.

This exercise from Rolfing Movement teaches you how to envision your goals coming towards you. All the people you will meet are as eager to meet you as you are to meet them. Immediately, your perceived effort is cut in half because your goals are meeting you halfway. Plus, seeing those people in your future, albeit in imagination, makes the goals feel easier, more achievable and builds your confidence. Confident people achieve more because they believe they can.

1. Walk at an easy pace.
2. Look at the horizon.
3. Imagine the foreground coming toward you as you move.
4. Notice the change in your pace: Have you slowed down? Are your heels striking softer? Is it easier to walk?
5. Practice until it feels natural to walk this way.
6. Imagine your goals coming toward you. Imagine a crowd of people cheering and running toward you, like fans waiting at the finish line. They celebrate your win, they admire and love you to where you feel cherished.
7. Do at bedtime to program your subconscious to make new cells with the necessary confidence, strength and determination to bring your goals to fruition; when you change emotionally, so does your DNA.

"It's pleasing to discover that it isn't necessary to drive oneself forward; instead, one can simply allow oneself to move forward as blocks are removed. Thus, one becomes attracted by the future rather than propelled by the past."
– **David R. Hawkins**, *Along the Path of Enlightenment*

Joy of Being Creative

To increase energy, awareness and belonging.

Art projects bring calm and a respite from upheaval. In the act of creating, you are in the present. These can be simple, short projects, or more complicated ones. You choose what works best for you. Even if you don't think you're artistic, try some activities with friends or take a class. Doing art projects is known to be therapeutic plus they can be fun.

> *"The process of creativity and genius is inherent in human consciousness. As every human has within himself the same essence of consciousness, so is genius a potential that resides within everyone. It simply waits for the right circumstance to express itself."*
> – **David R. Hawkins**, *Along the Path to Enlightenment*

Summary

How you handled life got you to where you are today. You decided you wanted a better life and began a journey to reinvent yourself. To change meant you had to learn new skills. In this chapter you learned that happiness is fickle, and that joy can be learned. You determined which level of reality you currently live in and which level you need to live in to achieve your goals. You learned that adding intention to your actions made them exponentially more powerful. You learned that walking backward and skipping enlivened your body and elevated you to joy. You learned that listening to an audiobook increased relaxation and improved your sleep. You learned the immediate mood boost of exchanging smiles and hugging people. You started your day energized with twenty minutes of meditation, twenty minutes of inspirational reading and twenty minutes of exercising. You learned exercises to calm yourself and gain clarity.

Congratulations!

You have successfully completed another two elements of this journey. You have learned how to reinvent yourself into someone you admire, and thereby, create the marriage and life you want. You learned ways to regain calm, clarity, wisdom, grace, acceptance and willingness when beset by upheaval. You've learned new skills to make this journey easier.

You have finished J-O-U-R-N of your journey. You are more than halfway through. You have changed so much that you don't recognize yourself! I am so very proud of you. It takes courage to change. You have shown fortitude, grace, grit, and determination to get this far. Well done!

Chapter 9

E = Emancipation from Bad Habits

"**Y**ou can't afford the luxury of a negative thought" was the title of a book by Peter McWilliams. Negative thoughts are counterproductive. They bring you down into the chaos of destructive emotions. Destructive emotions are like quicksand; the more you think them, the deeper you sink. Shame, blame, grief, apathy, guilt, fear, anger, and pride weigh you down. These low-life friends got you to where you were when you bought this book.

> *"When we heal something in ourselves, we heal it for the world."*
> – **David R. Hawkins**, *Letting Go: The Pathway of Surrender*

Positive thoughts are like hot air balloons buoying you upwards and onward. Positive thoughts cleanse the muck from your mind and soul.

Courage introduces you to neutrality, willingness, acceptance, reason, love, and joy. Courage is the boisterous leader of this new clique of friends known as the untouchables. The lower emotions secretly want to be admitted into this bold group, but lack the necessary skills required to gain admittance.

Some people remain in pain regardless of being worked on by gifted practitioners, being seen by excellent doctors and taking medicine. They are addicted to pain. Pain is their identity. It is near impossible to help these people because they are not willing to change. To heal would mean to give up suffering. They wear pain like armor to shield themselves. The more they implode in pain, the more they hurt. These people have a history of falls, migraines and blaming others.

To thrive means to be your best self. It is way beyond safety and surviving. It is above enduring and enthusiasm. It is higher than adapting and accepting. It is even higher on the consciousness scale than forgiving, respect, and courage. It's when you begin to shine with inner joy.

Every day you have a choice: to thrive or not to thrive. Denial keeps you stuck in a loop of blaming others for your dissatisfaction with your marriage and your life. Denial blinds you from seeing that you are the driver of your life. Denial is like a blindfold. Until you have the courage to take off the blindfold, you run into walls and sinkholes, ravines and off cliffs. Until you have the willingness to give up drama and tragedy you remain slumming with the scum emotions of shame, guilt, grief, fear, anger, and pride.

> "[I]t is natural for the ego to be vain, greedy, hateful, prideful, resentful, envious, and more. These were learned accretions to the ego during its evolutionary development over eons of time. Therefore, it is not necessary to feel guilty because these primitive emotions merely need to be out-grown and discarded..."
> – **David R. Hawkins**, *Along the Path to Enlightenment*

In this chapter, you learn how to separate needs from wants. Wants are desires that distract you from your goal of a happy marriage and life. Desires lure like honey, but create a sticky mess. Needs are the advice from your new group of courageous friends. To leap from follower to leader is to rip off your blindfold and take control of your life. Going fast intensifies the speed bumps of life. The faster you go, the more damage results because you don't have the time to avoid the danger, to swerve around and avoid fights with your spouse. Learning to slow down to see that you create mayhem, that you perpetuate discord, changes not only you, but your relationship and everyone around you.

To learn to breathe into sour emotions rather than regurgitate them is like fixing a flat tire. Immediately you have the wherewithal to continue onward on your journey of creating a life of harmony. Every life has good times and bad times and needs a spare tire for those unexpected mishaps. Keeping an ace is like having one more skill to pull you up and out of derailing.

Change is not linear. It is a zigzag line of ups and downs. Growth happens in spurts. Mistakes and failures look like defeat, but are valuable teachers and part of your journey. They mentor you to jump back on the highway of reinventing yourself and forging a person you like and admire.

> "The benefit of accepting one's defects instead of denying them is an increase in an inner sense of self-honesty, security, and higher self-esteem, accompanied by greatly diminished defensiveness. A self-honest person is not prone to having his or her feelings hurt by others; therefore, honest insight has an immediate benefit in the reduction of actual, as well as potential, emotional pain."
> – **David R. Hawkins**, *Along the Path to Enlightenment*

Think bows and arrows. The further you pull the string back, the further the arrow flies. When you need to change your marriage and your life, you must pull back and take the time to learn new skills strong enough to create the change you need. Think mountain. When you started this book, you were in a valley looking up at an insurmountable mountain. This book guides you to find the secret passages through and over this rugged terrain called your life.

To stop looking over your shoulder at where you were instead of where you are going shifts your focus to positive. Think Groundhog Day. In this comedy, Bill Murray brilliantly demonstrated the frustration of not learning from his mistakes. His frustration was so great that he repeatedly tried to commit suicide because each day he fell into the same water-filled potholes. Not until he decided to live did he decide to learn from his mistakes and ultimately change his behavior.

Likewise, you have been on a journey to identify and understand your mistakes in your marriage and your life. Epiphanies only happen in moments of calm and are your best ace. They are quick and easy solutions to your biggest problems. They are like manna from heaven.

Old habits are hard to break. This chapter teaches fast ways to calm down when you inadvertently slide down into the quagmire of negativity. Looking right is one more way to uplift yourself and to calm down when life hits you over the head. Faking laughter until it happens spontaneously heals people from discord and disease. To commit to laughing fifteen minutes a day for forty days is a colonic that flushes the toxins of despair from your body, mind, and soul.

"Man extrapolates the ego's qualities to God and then fears God. Judgment Day is every day; it is already here and is constant and unending."
– **David R. Hawkins**, *Along the Path to Enlightenment*

Stop Blaming Others

A quantum leap in consciousness.

When you get angry or disgusted, and blaming others for your upset, look to see if you are upset at yourself. Take the other person out of the equation and look to see how you could have chosen something different. Stop being dramatic and thinking others have to change for you to be a better person. Stop thinking you have to make huge changes like divorcing or moving out to get what you want. Instead, assess what you need to do, or what level of consciousness you achieve, to bring your dreams to fruition. Often, your dreams are attainable as soon as you build bridges across the chasms of doubt, anger, pride, and shame.

"Should" is the red flag that you are doing something for others and not keeping integrity. Should is a moral judgment. It usually causes resentment, grudges, and even retaliatory behavior done out of spite. Think scraping nails on a chalkboard. Using the word should is like denigrating your husband to an ideal, not a man. You castrate his confidence. Instead, respect him the way you want and need to be respected and honored.

Needs versus Wants

To gain clarity.

Wants are fleeting fantasies of what might be fun to do or have or would make life easier or more enjoyable. Needs are the quintessential requirements for us to thrive.

1. Make a list of what you need.
2. Spend no more than fifteen minutes writing these down.
3. Cross off any that are wants, meaning not essential.
4. Post these where you see them daily.
5. Let your unconscious work on how easiest to attain these needs.

Leap from Passive Follower to Leader

To increase confidence and integrity.

A leader is someone who follows their ideas; a person willing to go outside the box of the norm. A leader is also a person who is brave enough to try new things, fail, try again, fail, and finally bring their dreams to fruition. It can be a group of one, just you alone. But surprisingly and unexpectedly, when you bring to light your ideas, there are people who like them. Even if it was never your goal to please others, often pleasing yourself results in pleasing or improving the lives of others.

"You don't have to be brave, but by the act of not giving up, you are being courageous."
   – David R. Hawkins, *Along the Path to Enlightenment*

Sometimes you give up just before you are about to succeed. Success stories often tell how people kept on after countless failures. For example, Colonel Sanders felt a failure, slept in the back seat of his car, and wanted to commit suicide at age sixty-five. But in writing his will he listed all the things he had wanted to do before he died and realized he was a good cook. He then cooked up chicken for customers and sold KFC for two million dollars at age seventy-three.

Slow Down

To increase calm and clarity.

Too often, you commit yourself to do too much. Sometimes you become so productive that your days are over-filled with work, children, gym, volunteering, social life, and play to where you don't have time to smile. Calm only happens when not rushing. Dedicate fifteen to thirty minutes each day to meditate or be still, a time when you're not planning activities and can simply breathe and be still. Notice your breathing. Allow the breath to get bigger and fuller and deeper. Deeper breaths quiet the body and rejuvenate the spirit. Sometimes epiphanies will bubble up about how to be more organized or an easier way to do your tasks, so your day flows more effortlessly. This quiet time will make you appreciate everything else in your life.

Emotional Flat Tire

To restore equanimity.

"Acceptance is the great healer of strife, conflict, and upset. It also corrects major imbalances of perception and precludes the dominance of negative feelings. Everything serves a purpose. Humility means that we will not understand all events or occurrences. Acceptance is not passivity, but non-positionality."
– **David R. Hawkins**, *Along the Path to Enlightenment*

It is easy to confuse acceptance with resignation or "being a doormat," a way to keep peace. In truth, capitulating comes from the fear of upsetting others and a hope that things will get better. You can live a long time on hope, but at some point resentments build until they threaten suffocation, and it's too late to clean up all that had unwittingly been agreed to by remaining silent.

Breathe into this, whatever this is.

Big breaths inflate you when you feel deflated my life. Usually when upset, your breath becomes shallow making it harder to adapt or think clearly, much less thrive. Breathing is fundamental to being alive, and in truth, the bigger the breath, the more alive you feel.

By not describing your upset, you neither narrow your focus nor limit the volume of your breath. Words limit your thinking. The more words you use to describe your upset only fuels your upset into becoming bigger than it began. You create a mountain out of a potato. Upheaval causes harm to your wellbeing and tension with those around you. You arrogantly believe it's your right to spew your opinions blinded by your pride to not see your limited thinking and mean-spiritedness.

"The realization that there is a source of joy and happiness that is beyond the ego is a major step."
   – **David R. Hawkins**, *Along the Path to Enlightenment*

The mind goes off on these tangents unaware of all the other options, unaware that many other emotions are happening simultaneously. Because the responses are full of dismay, anger, fear, shame, and guilt, the mind works to explain what cannot be explained, especially in natural disasters like hurricanes. The breathing goes shallow, and the body goes into mourning.

"Breathe into this, whatever this is" invites breath into the body. It allows the mind to go silent instead of becoming agitated. Using the word "this" invites breath into everything that is being felt. A wide range of emotions is happening at the same instant, most of which are not in awareness. As the chest expands with each breath, calmness quiets the upset and there is a willingness to see everything, most surprisingly to see that there is joy amongst the sadness, horror, and pain. Without words defining your experience, you stay below language and are then able to enjoy each moment. Without any judgment, without any agenda, and without any right or wrong, life has drama, but you are no longer a part of the drama. Life is so much more than its horrors. As soon as words are assigned, such as horrible, mean, wrong or bad, only those emotions come to the forefront. Only those emotions are the ones you feel and believe apply to the situation.

Breathing inflates what sour emotions deflate.

By repeating the mantra, "Breathe into this, whatever this is," you see and feel all the other emotions circling such as confusion, compassion, courage, acceptance, joy, and peace. Yes, even amidst tragedy, joy, and peace still flourish as an option.

Someone wise said, "God is not in the acts that happen, but in your response to them." Too often, you inflict the tragedy onto your body and sink with it. It's like going down into the rabbit hole where everything is denser and darker. The lighter words float out of sight, unnoticed, and forgotten. Whereas the more you say this mantra, "Breathe into this, whatever this is," the more the heavier emotions evaporate and no longer weigh you down. You are left with the lighter, life-supporting emotions such as courage, acceptance, love, joy, and peace.

Focusing on "all" is to forego focusing on failures. This mantra is not a shield against pain, but rather a buoy to keep you afloat above the harsh emotions. Breath is the universal buoy, which inflates you back to who you are so that you can shine even during hard times. By buoying yourself, you can help buoy others to inflate back to who they are.

"[A]ll suffering and emotional pain result from resistance."
– David R. Hawkins, *Along the Path to Enlightenment*

Pain is a shock to the psyche and body. The more you dwell on it, the more it hurts. "Breathe into this, whatever this is" distracts you to focus on only this single moment and not on the pain. It brings life where you had felt death. By accepting what you don't like, you are no longer deflated by it. "Breathe into this, whatever this is" inflates the flat tire of your aggrieved psyche and reminds you of the infinite gentler, kinder options from which to choose. Wisdom knows that what you feel is always a choice.

Letting go is quite different than resignation. There is no doormat in letting go. It takes courage and strength to let go for a void ensues and you have no idea what will fill it. It's not a gamble. That would be simpler and safer for you'd know the gain and loss. In letting go you release to spirit, to the unknown, opening yourself to the seemingly chaotic ricochet of the cosmos, trusting that balance will prevail. Open and vulnerable, you feel raw. It's the epitome of alive, and somehow you realize you've looped back into joy and the world is good again.

Anytime, anywhere and with anyone this mantra restores calm.

Mantra—"Breathe into this, whatever this is."

- When upset, inhale, and repeat the mantra.
- For several breaths, inhale repeating the mantra.
- Allow the lungs to expand bigger with each breath.
- Notice if the shoulders drop and the mind eases.
- Notice if you become aware of more than the initial thought of sadness, frustration, anger, or overwhelm, etc.
- Notice your chest. Does it feel heavier or lighter?
- Notice your mood. Does it feel heavier or lighter?
- What other changes are happening in your body?

Keep an Ace

To uplift yourself when you slip into negativity.

Everyone has ups and downs. Bad days happen to good people. It does not matter if you are rich or poor, young or old, male or female. They happen to all races, nationalities, and religions. But so often you think you should be able to drive through life on autopilot and get offended when things go awry. You would never drive with your eyes closed. You drive on the lookout for unexpected danger: potholes, debris, animals, and swerving cars. You keep tools in the trunk or have a membership for roadside service. You expect trouble and are prepared for it. Yet in marriage and life, you are less prepared and often caught off-guard, almost surprised that inconvenience much less tragedy happens.

Keeping an ace "up your sleeve" is a way to ensure you have help to turn to when needed. Everyone needs someone to turn to. Having someone neutral and 100 percent supportive means you have a reliable resource for encouragement and guidance. Just making the call or prayer can be reassuring.

It's too easy to get sucked into the quagmire of fear, overwhelm, or bitterness. Just the act of doing something positive breaks the loop of panic. Once no longer panicked you can begin to take whatever actions are possible to mitigate or adapt to the problem. An ace is like insurance. Having it handy at all times gives you more confidence that when bowled over by life, you still have a soft place to land. Ultimately, in short, that you will triumph over disaster.

Stop Looking in the Rear-view Mirror

To look forward instead of at the past.

Too much of your time is spent reminiscing, bitter that the past was better then than now, or over regrets and resentments about what happened or should have happened, about your mistakes, or about your losses, missed opportunities, and maybe most of all, about the stupid things you said or did that you wish you hadn't. Yet, each time you think about the past it robs you of doing something proactive and positive in the now which is the only time you have any control over.

Thus, each time you catch yourself reflecting on the past, consciously say (aloud or silently): "Thank you for being part of my past. Thank you for today and the chance to do life differently and in a way that brings better results." Do this as often as necessary.

Epiphanies

To channel your quiet voice.

Epiphanies are ideas that solve problems. They work for everyone involved. They seemingly come from nowhere, and just pop into your head. However, they only come when calm and focused in the present. They can happen driving, exercising, meditating, walking, cleaning, showering, or writing, but again, only while calm and enjoying the moment with a quiet mind.

Slow down. Bumps in the road, and also in life, hurt worse the faster you're going. In contrast, going slower makes the bumps easier to handle. Going slow increases your calm, clarity and willingness because you are not rushing or worried. Brilliance only happens when you get out of your way and channel your quiet voice. Your quiet voice only speaks in epiphanies. These succinct directives are always available as long as you are calm enough to hear them. They are like hearing the voice of God.

> *"Traditionally, the relinquishment of the ego's programs has been described as arduous and difficult, requiring many lifetimes to accomplish. On the contrary, a profound humility and the willingness to surrender all to God at great depth make it possible for the transition to occur in a split second. Thus, the pathway to enlightenment may be viewed as a slow process or a sudden one."*
> – **David R. Hawkins**, *Along the Path to Enlightenment*

Looking Right Is Calming

To gain clarity and wisdom.

Holding conversations with yourself is an exercise to hear exactly what you need and want to hear. Contrary to the popular joke that you're going crazy when you start answering yourself, it is grand to hear unabashed praise, affection, and tenderness. To hear what you crave to hear instantly cheers you. It is like never being alone. It is like being companioned by a constantly positive person who adores you. It is like hearing Jesus give you kind words of love.

Breaking negative thinking makes you feel better and gives instant relief. Too often, negative thinking is like being caught in a riptide, and if unchecked, can lead to a panic attack. Having a quick ace to stop you from drifting helplessly along in negative thoughts is like buoy of salvation. It brings you back to safety.

The benefit of this technique is that you counsel yourself by accessing the two hemispheres of your brain. You access the left brain by looking left at the ten o'clock position of a clock. You access the right brain by looking right at the two o'clock position. Looking left channels the negative side of your thoughts which frets about your past and future. Looking right channels the positive side of your thinking which is always in the present moment.

Having one person completely understand you and still like you is like manna from heaven. To hear advice from the part of you that is not judgmental, caustic, easily offended or fearful is to get in touch with the sane part of you. To meet that part of yourself that likes you is like making a new best friend.

1. Imagine yourself looking at a huge analog clock the size of a building.
2. Look up at the ten o'clock position and ask, "What do you need to tell me?"
3. Listen.
4. Look up at the two o'clock position and ask, "What do you need to tell me?"
5. Listen.
6. Compare the two. Are they different? Which voice do you like better?
7. Which voice makes you feel better about yourself?

This technique is a fast way to tap into the negative beliefs that live under your consciousness like a riptide. That riptide is not dangerous unless you slip into its stream. Swimmers are taught that you cannot swim against a riptide, but must swim at an angle to escape its current. Likewise, when you want to escape negative thinking it is fastest to angle toward positive thinking.

Understanding that dangerous emotions swim in your unconscious is like seeing the sharks lurking there threatening to gobble you up. These sharks are called shame, guilt, grief, fear, anger, and pride. Seeing that gushingly positive emotions swim in your unconscious is like seeing the dolphins who ram sharks until they bleed (and are then eaten by other sharks) and to realize that you are not defenseless, that your strong friends called courage, neutrality, willingness, acceptance, reason, love and joy are the only creatures who can rescue you from an attack of the sharks.

> *"Courage implies the willingness to try new things and to deal with the vicissitudes of life. At this level of empowerment one is able to cope with and effectively handle the opportunities of life. There is the capacity to face fears or character defects and to grow despite them, and anxiety does not cripple endeavor as it does at the lower stages of evolution."*
> – **David R. Hawkins**, *Along the Path to Enlightenment*

Fun Tip: This technique can be done while driving; however, instead of looking askance think "ten o'clock" and "two o'clock" and hear the condemning tirade of the first and gushing accolade of the latter. Once you have mastered this skill, when you just want a fast pick-me-up repeat saying "two o'clock" twenty times and notice the calming effect.

When feeling in a funk or in need of a better perspective:

- List five beliefs about yourself.
- Begin each with "I am…"
- Start with whatever comes to mind, however silly.
- Often the list will start with beliefs that lack confidence.
- Be willing for the beliefs to become bolder as your determination and resolve to build like a fire burning brighter.
- List ten more positive beliefs from this level of increased confidence.
- Continue listing empowering beliefs until confidence is restored and you can resume working on your goals.

For example, here is a list of beliefs that a client wrote when feeling down.

1. I am stupid.
2. I am dumb.
3. I am resistant to being happy.
4. I am determined to become happy.
5. I am eager to find joy.
6. I am determined to have epiphanies to come up with ways that I would otherwise never think of.

You can see the progression of working through her self-loathing and regaining the levity and courage of higher levels of consciousness. This process is a zip line to feeling better.

Fight the Funk & Win

To gain clarity and wisdom.

Funks come out of nowhere, triggered by something as simple as hearing a song. Rather than beat yourself up for slipping down a long slide, wrest this beast by listing your levels of consciousness at that moment. The following is an excerpt from a client's journal:

1. Shame—I hate myself. I am no good. I am awful.
2. Guilt—I have done so many bad things that I can hardly sleep.
3. Apathy—Who cares. It hurts too much to care.
4. Grief—Will these tears never stop? I am drowning.
5. Fear—I am dying.
6. Desire—I want to make so much money that my dad will be proud of me and I can remodel my home and buy a second home close to my kids and travel the world.
7. Anger—I hate everybody. They are all nuts.
8. Pride—I have worked hard and deserve to be respected.
9. Courage—[Big breath] Wow, life is expanding in new and wonderful ways that scare and excite me.
10. Neutrality—There is no right or wrong or good or bad. I am as I am, and other people are as they are.
11. Willingness—[Big breath] Okay, I am willing to do what I need to do without knowing the effect that I will have.
12. Acceptance—[Huge breath] I accept that God has a plan for me, specific tasks assigned that must be done before he recalls me to Heaven.
13. Reason—[Huge breath] I understand that I cannot and probably will never understand why people do what they do and that it is not my job or task to divine such.
14. Love—[Enormous breath] My heart swells the size of the planet for everyone and everything.
15. Joy—[Smile lights up whole body and soul] Yes. Yes. Yes. I am who I am and as God chooses me to be.

16. Peace—[Gasp] No, not ready God. I want to cry. I'm so sorry that this is not for me or I am still too dense to achieve this level.

17. Enlightenment—[Hold breath] Yep, waiting for this until at your side.

Life often feels like playing Chutes and Ladders, the child's game where if you land on a slide you have to slide down, sometimes back to the beginning of the game. It feels out of your control, a game of chance that the dice determined whether you lost or won the game. Yet like life, the game is to keep rolling the dice and moving forward. If you played long enough, you would reach the end.

Life is similar. Playing life offensively is to keep going even when it looks like there is no way to win. There is always a way to win. You just have to redefine winning. Often perfect looks different than you imagined.

Fun Tips:

1. In bed as you fall asleep, say each word as you inhale and slowly exhale, "Courage, neutrality, willingness, acceptance, reason, love, joy, peace, enlightenment." Notice if your breaths get bigger. Notice if your body relaxes. Notice if you are smiling.

2. When fatigued and need a boost of energy and clarity, say each word as you slowly inhale and slowly exhale, "Courage, neutrality, willingness, acceptance, reason, love, joy, peace, enlightenment." Notice if your breaths get bigger. Notice if your body relaxes. Notice if you are smiling. Notice if your mind cleared and your energy increased.

Fake Laughter Until It's Real

To trick your body into feeling good.

Fifteen minutes of continuous laughter gives a similar euphoria to a "runner's high." Scientific studies proved that laughing for just ten minutes reaped health benefits from immediate to long-term. Norman Cousins, an American journalist and author, healed himself from several acute illnesses using laughter.

> *"I made the joyous discovery that ten minutes of genuine belly laughter had an anesthetic effect and would give me at least two hours of pain-free sleep."*
>
> **– Norman Cousins**

Some scientific studies proving laughter is good medicine:

Stanford University (by Dr. William F. Fry, psychiatrist) showed that even faked laughter reaped health benefits. Loma Linda University Medical Center (California) by Dr. Lee Berk, Ph.D. found that the group of heart patients who laughed improved on all levels. Dr. Hunter (Patch) Adams, M.D. inspired hospitals to recognize that "healing should be a loving human interchange not a business transaction." He inspired that clowns be allowed in hospitals as therapy. Dr. Madan Kataria, M.D. (a medical doctor in India) was writing an article "Laughter-The Best Medicine" and as part of his research started what is now called Laughter Yoga. What began as a group of five people in a park in Mumbai in 1995 has swiftly evolved into thousands of Laughter Yoga Clubs in over sixty-five countries. Dr. Kataria and his wife (Madhuri Kataria, co-founder of Laughter Yoga) both were yoga practitioners and noticed the similarities between laughing and yoga exercises, both get the body moving and breathing more deeply.

What you think is like the steering wheel to your moods. You don't even have to believe something for it to make you feel bad. Therefore, saying "Ha-ha-ha-ha-ha-ha" stops negative thinking. Even better, if you say it while grinning, you will soon feel much better! If grinning seems too hard, hold a pen or pencil in your mouth. This engages the muscles used for smiling.

Forty-Day Challenge To Laugh

To increase levity and health.

Back for a seventh year in China, I was annoyed by the chatter of a language I didn't speak, stared at because I was a foreigner, long lines, people pushing, severe pollution, constant demolition and construction of streets and buildings, pervasive filth, and no hot water in our apartment. Family seemed on the other side of the world, and ten months a prison sentence. My usual motto of "I'm only a phone call away" seemed glib. Why was I still here? Because I hadn't come up with any better ideas.

Granted, I was so tired after a twenty-four-hour trip that I didn't unpack my toothbrush. After watching a little television, I slept for twelve hours. Sometime during the night, I decided I had to change my attitude and vowed to laugh for fifteen minutes per day for forty days. I dropped the goals to lose weight and exercise, but maybe they would happen just because I was happier. And maybe if I just laughed more, my relationship would be more fun and my life more satisfying.

1. Decide to be proactive about being happy.
2. Laugh fifteen consecutive minutes per day for forty days.
3. Record the experience.
4. Only post successes.

Day One: New things immediately began to happen. Laughter got rid of my gloom and made me glad to be back in China. It also became the crux of making every moment better to the point of starting a website www.Joy-for-DUMMIES.com.

Day Two: I feel like such a dummy for slipping back into gloom and doom so often, for not appreciating and being grateful, for I've always had more than most people, more love, more opportunities, more money, and I love my job teaching tenth graders, love living in China, which is why I called the website Joy for Dummies. Who knows? Maybe I can turn this into a book published by the "for Dummies" series?

Day Sixteen: My relationship is more fun and playful. My ability to stay calm while doing frustrating things like setting up a new website and blog has increased. The ever-present annoyance from being numb for five years is greatly diminished. My constant sneezing is gone! Sorted boxes that were in storage for three years! Sleeping better and able to sleep without listening to meditative tapes. Silent laughter is a great way to start the day! I'm laughing through mishaps like being locked out of my apartment and water leaking under the cooler. I'm more confident and less bored, almost no negative chatter!

Chronicling my forty-days began as a way to stay accountable, ensuring that I would complete the challenge, but soon the results were so uplifting that I was eager to share my experiences.

I've dealt with depression off and on since age fourteen. I've tried dozens of modalities,

been to numerous therapists, read upwards of 100 self-help books, and tried anti-depressants. I've had stress so bad it caused amnesia and been catatonic as a teen, and as an adult blood oozed from the pores of my arms and legs, and I also had seizure-threatening high blood pressure, stress-induced asthma, and panic attacks.

Being happy became a quest. My moods changed so quickly that I didn't trust myself. Even my teachers at Rolfing school couldn't agree whether I was an introvert or an extrovert, until one brilliantly explained, "She is both, depends on her mood."

For many years, I couldn't be happy unless everyone around me was happy. But pleasing others proved to only stockpile resentments. It confused and angered my loved ones that I hadn't stood up for myself. But pleasing myself seemed to annoy or anger them, and I truly didn't like being alone, so it seemed better to adapt and hope that I'd be happy.

However, walking out of long-term relationships, including two marriages, caused grief for us all, and I was determined to make my current relationship work, especially since it was the best of my life.

Noticing that he laughed easily with others, but not with me, I decided I needed to learn how to laugh and searched on the internet. That's when I found Laughter Yoga. Laughter Yoga was built on the premise that the body doesn't know the difference between real and fake laughter, if done willingly, and thus the body gets the same physiological and psychological benefits. Thus, you don't need a sense of humor. In fact, they almost guarantee you'll laugh doing their unique concept.

No therapy had ever made me laugh, so I signed up for a class. Three hundred dollars seemed cheap for two days of laughing. In addition, it appealed to me to get a certificate to become a Laughter Yoga Leader. The idea of making money teaching others to laugh made me laugh. Just signing up to take this class made my husband laugh, too.

Why is it important to make only positive statements?

Because it feels good to succeed. Focusing on how you have failed makes you feel bad. Change happens with baby steps. Usually your expectations are bigger than your achievements. Also, feeling good gives you more energy, so it empowers you to take more baby steps. Too often, you don't even try most things, because you assume you can't do it.

If you or your husband tended to feel shame in most everything, that made your marriage particularly tense and miserable. "Should have" is the red flag which indicates that you are blaming either yourself or someone else. Remember, shame is the lowest level of consciousness. All emotions are higher. Put a bag of frozen peas on your face to shock you out of this negative, highly destructive habit. Don't take a nice hot bath because that allows you to wallow in putrid thoughts. You must gently shock yourself to retrain the brain from going down those sabotaging paths.

Brené Brown explained the difference between shame and guilt as follows:

> *"Guilt = I did something bad.*
> *Shame = I am bad.*
> *Shame is about who we are, and guilt is about our behaviors."*

Sex Is Important

To enhance intimacy.

It is the rare marriage that is happy without a good sex life. Orgasms are the exclamation points in life. Most everybody likes the deep relaxation that follows. They like being so in the moment that nothing else exists. The world narrows to just you. Time feels like it stops. Many people like the rise of excitement, the jubilant cresting, and the gentle cascade coming down from this peak. They revel in contentment of exhausted bliss.

If you do not enjoy sex, you are missing out on one of life's pleasures to be human. Only highly conscious beings do intercourse for the fun of it. Intervention is needed. There can be many reasons why sex is not enjoyable. You need to teach your husband how to pleasure you. You cannot assume that he knows what to do. You must guide him, experiment with different positions, be playful, and make it fun and sexy. If being sexy feels wrong, then you need to let go of shame.

> *"To undo shame, it is helpful to realize that it is based on pride."*
> – **David R. Hawkins**, *Along the Path to Enlightenment*

Problems also happen when you do not like the smell of your husband. Pheromones are real. Not everyone smells the same. The chemistry between the two of you must match or else his breath smells bad regardless of how much mouthwash he uses. When you don't like how he smells, and I'm talking about fresh out of a shower, you won't like how you smell on him. When a couple is well-suited even morning breath does not smell bad because you have a similar chemistry.

Joy emanates from deep within the pelvis. In women, the wellspring of joy is in the area of the uterus. In men, the wellspring is in the area of the prostate. Removal of said organ does not eliminate joy, but often dampens it. However, visualizing that the organ is still there will restore its vitality. Just like some amputees feel pain in a limb no longer there, joy can be restored into the area of the removed uterus or prostate.

How to Cure Insomnia

To sleep deeper and more soundly.

Sleep is important. If you or your husband suffered from insomnia, that added a huge stress to your marriage. Tired people are grumpy. Tired people are hard to live with. Tired people have less resiliency and thus are usually easy to upset. Whenever overwhelmed, lay down for a nap. Fifteen minutes of rest can calm you down. If you're crying, put yourself to bed. Rested, problems are easier to handle.

Listening to meditation music (kept on all night at low volume) is soothing white noise which allows the mind to ignore other sounds like a ticking clock, sounds from the street, or your husband's snoring. It's designed to put you in an alpha state which is relaxing and regenerative. It's a lullaby for adults. You may find you sleep sounder, too, for you're less likely to be awakened by incidental noises.

Listening to a book on tape (kept on low all night) also works. Being read a story is like being a kid again. Use a book with a melodious voice and that is not too interesting. I listened to Power vs. Force over one hundred times because his voice was deep and soothing. Plus, each sentence is instructive, so hearing a few sentences during the night was like hearing just what I needed to hear.

Repeating "Ha-ha-ha-ha-ha-ha-ha-ha-ha" silently but with your mouth open also works because it stops the hamster-wheel chatter. Thinking of things past, present or future makes you restless and unable to sleep. By repeating "Ha-ha-ha-ha-ha-ha-ha-ha" for several breaths, you'll become calm, relaxed, and soon fall back to sleep.

Remembering dreams can work, too. Again, because it accesses what you experienced while sleeping. It doesn't matter if the dream was recent or long ago, or if you can only remember pieces of it. This keeps you resting, whereas if you begin to list what you have to do, or begin to worry, or to think of some past bad memory, you become agitated. Thinking of any and all dreams you can remember puts you back into a dream-state.

Remember, just lying still with the mind quiet, your body is resting. It is almost as restorative as sleeping, so stop fretting and start resting better! If your husband objects to hearing music or listening to a book, wear earbuds. This has the double advantage of acting as earplugs which helps to muffle sounds like his snoring.

Drink a glass of warm or cold milk at bedtime, or in the middle of the night, but I gained weight doing this option, so I prefer the above options. Milk works because it has tryptophan in it which is an amino acid that increases relaxation.

Read at bedtime. Reading relaxes the brain and stops incessant chatter that's keeping you awake. Within five to fifteen minutes you will usually be able to fall back asleep. However, your book can't be too interesting. Try reading something technical or, if you're a student, a textbook.

Take a hot shower or bath. Water often reverses how you feel. When sleepy, a shower wakes you up and makes going to work easier. It works in the opposite direction. When you're not able to sleep, a shower relaxes you. A relaxed body sleeps more deeply, meaning you get a sounder sleep.

Imagination is another way to relax yourself. Imagine if money were no object, what you would do. Let your mind envision glorious things you'd buy or places you'd go, and give as many details as you can. Let your mind imagine big. Do this until you drift back to sleep.

Breathing out feelings is another way to relax. Take a big breath and say some feeling as you exhale. To the extent that feeling is causing you stress is to the extent you will get a release. For example, say "worried" and exhale. Notice if you feel more relaxed. Try "tired" and notice how much your body lets go. Try "exhausted," "sad," "angry," and so on. You can try your husband's or children's names, even food. If not getting much of a release, try "happy" or "excited." Yes, excitement can keep you awake, a good problem, but it still hinders your sleep. It can be interesting to see what feelings are keeping you keyed up. This also is getting you to take deep breaths which helps to relax your body and mind. It is a way to discharge pent up energy that you probably had little awareness of having. If this method works, you will feel a bigger intake of breath on words that relax you, followed by a noticeable letting go.

Remember, lying still with eyes closed is resting your body. The quieter the mind, the better the body rests. The more relaxed the mind, the better the body rests.

Epsom Salts Baths

To ease the body, mind and soul.

A long soak in a hot bath is a remedy that eases tension. Adding Epsom salts (magnesium sulfate) to the water quadruples the effectiveness of tap water. Epsom salts can be purchased at grocery stores or pharmacies or in bulk at Costco. The body strives to equalize the level of salt outside of the body, thereby initiating fluids to move within the tissue. This movement dissipates stiffness and soreness, flushes lactic acid from your muscles and flushes toxins from your body. Toxins come from tension, fighting, fatigue, worry, anger, caffeine and sugar, to name a few. Toxins harden muscles and cause knots, headaches and cramps.

If you're stiff and sore from muscle exertion or a fall, or are fighting the flu, or have a sinus or chest infection, or are too wired to sleep, or are in need of a general tonic, soaking in an Epsom salts bath is an easy, quick remedy that at a minimum will be the equivalent of a relaxing massage. Because it's in the comfort of your home, you can do it at three in the morning. If you can't sleep due to restlessness or illness, soak in an Epsom salts bath to calm your body and brain.

1. Fill the tub with water as hot as is comfortable.
2. Pour in two cups of Epsom salts.
3. Stir until crystals dissolve.
4. Soak a minimum of ten minutes.
5. Longer is better, but results happen within ten minutes.
6. Can be repeated up to three times in one day.

Stop Humble Bragging

To stop irritating your husband.

Beware of this new oxymoron that happens so often it's been given a name. While humble people never brag and braggarts are not humble, humble bragging is when you're not trying to brag, but you are. For example, this client needed her eyes opened wide for what she thought was being nice was in reality obnoxious. "Every time my husband's ex comes to visit, I stay out of sight because his kids like me better than her. Can you imagine that? They like me better than their own mom. I don't want to make her feel bad, but they whine to sit on my lap, so I find it's best just to stay in the kitchen. You'd think they'd want to sit on her lap. They don't get to see her very often, gosh, you'd think she'd scoop them up. She's not much fun, so guess that's why the kids like me. I told the kids I'd bake lemon snowflakes, my mama's recipe, if they were nice to their mama. It's the kids' favorite cookie."

While her intent was to be considerate and helpful, by telling everyone what she did, she was making a big deal about it. She pointed out that she was the favorite, and more annoyingly, that she knew best how to handle his kids and his ex-wife. In essence, she was proclaiming that she was a better person. This insulted the ex-wife, turned the kids against their mom, made people take sides, and put the husband in an awkward position.

This is an example of how pride inflates the ego and swells the head. A more gracious woman would be inconspicuous in her efforts to maintain equanimity in this difficult situation. While her husband may think it was cute and was pleased that his kids liked her better, he was caught in the middle and thrust into mediating between his ex and his new wife. Sometimes statements like this are said as an offhand joke, and the woman thinks she is being funny, when in fact she is being tiresome and petty.

Both Harvard and the University of North Carolina Chapel Hill conducted a series of experiments. "Researchers established that there are two distinct types of humblebrags. The first falls back on a complaint ('I hate that I look so young; even a 19-year-old hit on me!') while the second relies on humility ('Why do I always get asked to work on the most important assignment?').

"The researchers then carried out experiments to see how people responded to humblebrags, with a particular focus on the bragger's perceived likability and competence. They found that regular bragging was better on both counts, because it at least comes off as genuine, Sezer says. Even complainers were more likable and seemed more competent than humblebraggers of any type.

"If you want to announce something, go with the brag and at least own your self-promotion and reap the rewards of being sincere, rather than losing in all dimensions," Sezer says.

"Better yet, she says, get somebody else to "wingman" your boasting. 'If someone brags for you, that's the best thing that can happen to you, because then you don't seem like you're bragging," Sezer says."

Beware of being nice. Being nice is taking care of other people's needs at your own expense. It leads to resentment. It leads to exhaustion because you're giving and not receiving. You can be generous, thoughtful, polite, and compassionate; however you must never be nice. Nice is like lying. It's a form of humblebragging. You mean well, but are saying you know best what others need and that your superpowers are so great that you can do it all, and that you have no needs. Nice is patronizing, asserting that you know how to take care of them better than they know how to take care of themselves.

Always keep boundaries to ensure that you are taking care of yourself. Say no when being imposed upon. Say yes only when it works for you. Being a martyr only obligates everyone else to take care of you, and can make you feel like you're entitled to adoration because they owe you gratitude. Can you see how these are low-level emotions? By raising your consciousness to higher levels, grace shows up in your demeanor and your health improves. You look years younger and have more energy.

"I knew a woman who went about bragging of her troubles, so, of course, she always had something to brag about."
— Florence Scovel Shinn

Summary

You learned that your needs are more important than your wants, and that by taking care of your needs, you take care of yourself. Wants are merely desires and do not support you or your family. In fact, they lead to mayhem when overly indulged, such as buying more clothes than you need, a better house or car than needed, or expensive toys that gather dust.

You learned how to switch from being a follower to becoming a leader. In order to gain respect, you must assert yourself. If you're not in control, you're being controlled. Slow down enough to grow calm and clear-headed. Clarity builds confidence, emboldens you to try what you need to try, and allows you to hear your quiet voice. Hearing the quiet voice is like streaming consciousness, downloading the wisdom of the universe. It is to be in what's commonly called 'the flow' meaning things happen with synchronicity and ease.

You learned that looking right is calming. You learned that it's important to keep an ace, a quick way to restore your calm. You learned that laughing increases vitality and clear thinking. By vigilantly raising yourself back up to higher levels of consciousness, you stop looking backwards. Your focus is to make a future that reflects who you truly are, to do what you came on the planet to do, and to fulfill God's will.

Congratulations! You rid yourself of bad habits and learned better, more powerful ways to get the life you want. You are a calmer, wiser, more confident person who is clear about whether divorce is right for you. You see harmony and strength in your future. You know where you're headed and how to get there.

Take a moment to let all that you have learned sink in. Acknowledge how much you have grown and how hard you have worked. Revel in your newfound peace, clarity, willingness, and courage.

You are amazing! Well done!

Chapter 10

Y = You Love Your Decision

*Y*ou worked through despair and reinvented yourself. Think kiln. You began as a lump of clay, shaped and reshaped until you molded yourself into an artwork that delighted you. Think porcelain. Porcelain is fired at the highest temperatures of pottery. You went through fire to surrender your ego and be emancipated from old habits. You are fine china, exquisitely you. You integrated all that you learned and sculpted yourself into someone you like and admire. You have the courage to be outrageously you. You recognize that not everyone will applaud you, however you willingly go forward into your new life. Harmony reigns in your relationships with others and with yourself. You understand that you have all the skills you need to face new challenges. You love yourself unconditionally just as God does. You feel complete that this part of your journey is over. You trust that you can weather future storms, recognize that storms are a part of living, and see yourself as a perfect being, part of a perfect world. God is your mentor and friend. God walks beside you and holds your hand.

Tired of being a caterpillar?

Caterpillars are a metaphor for life. They go from creeping to winged; they morph from heavy to light, and from staying on one bush or tree to flying as far as 2,500 miles. They even go blind in the transition of molting a new skin. Caterpillars slough four or five skins, and eat their previous skins. While their DNA is programmed with everything it needs to become a butterfly or moth, it must eat voraciously to complete each metamorphosis.

Are you as determined as a caterpillar? Most people are born with all that they need to live. But like caterpillars, you must slough your skins when they are too tight. You must surrender narrow or negative thoughts and emotions that limit your growth and destroy you. Pride, anger, shame, guilt, apathy, grief, lust, and fear all cause more harm than good.

Change is often scary and hard. Yet, it begins with a resolve to trade your status quo for a newer, lighter, easier, more satisfying, and ultimately happier life. When you have the courage and willingness to surrender the ego, and to live with uncertainty and spontaneity, you can more easily decide which path you need to take.

However, like the caterpillar, you must enrich yourself with the necessary nutrients in order to grow steadily. Change happens in stages. By sloughing old ideas, opinions, beliefs, and expectations, you create space for new ideas, new opinions, new beliefs, and new expectations. Each phase is progress. Each time you triumph on some small baby step, your confidence grows a little bit bigger and little bit stronger. Meditation is like building a chrysalis, going inward to create a safe place to transform yourself. It is during meditation that you can practice having the relationship you want. It is in calm moments that you can see the changes you need to make to save your marriage, or gain the clarity to see that while painful, divorce is your best option.

Life is hard even for caterpillars. Weather, insects, carnivorous caterpillars, and birds all threaten and put caterpillars at risk. Eighty percent don't make it to become moths or butterflies. But unlike caterpillars, you have more control over your life. You have a brain and resources far beyond the caterpillar. The average lifespan of a human is six to nine decades, so you have time to shed many more skins. More than anything, you have the choice to grow or not to grow. This is the question you face every moment of every day.

Fun Fact: After a caterpillar sheds a skin, it swallows a lot of air to puff up as big as possible before that skin hardens, giving it more room to grow before it needs to shed again.

> *"Honest insight has an immediate benefit in the reduction of actual as well as potential emotional pain. A person is vulnerable to emotional pain in exact relationship to the degree of self-awareness and self-acceptance.*
>
> *"The key to painless growth is humility, which amounts to merely dropping pridefulness and pretense, and accepting fallibility as a normal human characteristic of self and others."*
> – **David R. Hawkins**, *Along the Path to Enlightenment*

Be gentle with yourself. Every day you are growing. Growing pains are real. Emotional pains often hurt more than physical pain. Take a deep breath so that you can swell into your best self. Fear, anger, grief, shame, apathy, guilt, and pride shut you down and blind you from seeing accurately and distort what you see. Every person has dips in their life. Highs and lows, celebrations and disappointments, and what sets people apart is whether they tend to loop or leap. Would you rather go around in circles, stewing over the same problems, and continue to have the same complaints? Or embark on a journey that improves the quality of your life?

> *"To pursue enlightenment in and*
> *of itself serves the world and God."*
> **– David R. Hawkins**, *Along the Path to Enlightenment*

What kind of person do you want to be? What would you do if you weren't afraid? It takes courage to do what brings you happiness when it causes others pain. Where is the fine line between caring for yourself and taking care of others? This line gets blurred and every person has a different definition.

Regardless of whether your circumstances are due to your actions or the result of external happenings, you always had a moment when you decided how to react. Sometimes it was so fast that you missed the moment of deciding, and before you knew it flew into a rage, or stomped off indignant, or turned your back, or dissolved into tears.

> *"The greatest teacher, failure is."*
> **– Yoda**, *The Last Jedi*

Have you ever read a self-help book only to feel shame that you weren't getting results? Or were ashamed that others were getting better results than you? This is normal. Sometimes you need someone to mentor you. Divorcing or repairing a difficult marriage is a scary and uncertain journey. To make changes is to morph into someone you don't know. Working with someone who has been down that road, and survived, can be of great help.

"Human progress is evolutionary, and therefore, mistakes and errors are inevitable. The only real tragedy is to become older but not wiser."

— **David R. Hawkins**, *Along the Path of Enlightenment*

Hiring a Life Coach

To make your journey easier.

Every marriage has its own set of landmines and obstacles, and sometimes an outsider can see more clearly how to resolve issues. Having someone validate that you're not crazy, that change is hard, and who encourages, offers new options, guides, empowers, and inspires can be the necessary extra component to getting you beyond the impasse of uncertainty and indecision.

Sometimes life is too much and the hurdles seem too high to jump. Overwhelm adds a new stress to where it clogs the brain and makes it almost impossible to be productive. Fear often follows, for if you can't do basic things, how will you take care of the kids? How will you pay the bills? How will you ever get through these hard times?

Sometimes you need a bit of help to bolster your courage and to understand what is bothering you. Sometimes you need the strength of another to validate that you're doing your best. You need a mentor, someone you trust and admire, who believes in you.

Why Hire a Life Coach?

Everyone needs support. A coach is different than a therapist. Therapists usually focus on why you have problems. Coaches focus on getting immediate results. Being accountable to a supportive person is empowering and uplifting. It reminds you that you're not alone. They help you get from A to Z without any analysis of why you feel the need to go from A to Z. They focus on building your future. You do not have to spend any time rehashing painful stories nor sharing any defeats or mistakes. There are no failures, only lessons to learn.

> *"The outer work can never be small if the inner work is great. And the outer work can never be great if the inner work is small."*
> – **Meister Eckhart**, *fourteenth-century Christian mystic*

How Does It Work?

The homework is simple and can be done when and where convenient for you. Meeting with the coach can be done in person or via phone or computer. Working with a life coach gets immediate results.

Who to Hire?

Life coaches are listed on the internet. It could be a friend or relative, but be careful, you don't want sympathy; you don't want rehashing any part of your past; you want accountability and to focus on where you want to go and what steps you are taking each day to get there. It is the rare friend or relative who can hold such a safe and sacred place to allow and nurture you to grow. Many friends and relatives love you with all their heart, yet feel threatened to see you change. They like you the way you are. They may not trust they will like you if you change.

Most people don't have the courage to change. You are going where you have never gone before, experiencing new emotions and probably as a result, new places, and meeting new people. Changing means going outside the safe zone of familiarity. Changing means letting go in the biggest ways, letting go of pain, letting go of heartache, letting go of seeing yourself as weak, stupid, too old, too fat, too poor, etc. Changing means giving up your identity.

But in reality, changing is stripping away the dead skin to reveal the parts underneath that are alive, vibrant, creative, confident, and calm. Change is often your only salvation. Doing new things breaks old patterns of belief. Learning new skills brings immediate confidence. If you can do one new thing, you are more likely to be able to do more new things. Baby steps grow into a whole new life.

Overwhelm and grief come in waves. Hiring a life coach is like picking up the pieces and moving on with someone at your side. It's a way to focus forward rather than living life looking in the rearview mirror at where you've been. Focusing on the past robs you of the present. Focusing on the past makes you think you cannot overcome present problems. Change can only happen in the present.

You finished one very important journey and now embark on another, the next chapter of your life. Life is a series of journeys. To thrive is to constantly evolve as you integrate new experiences. It is expanding your mind and soul every moment of every day for the rest of your life. Some journeys are hard and painful. Some journeys are fun and easy. All journeys require sloughing skins and growing new larger ones to fit the new you. Some journeys are done alone, such as exploring your mind and soul. Some journeys are done with others.

"The journey of a thousand miles begins with one step."
– Lao Tzu

Chapter 11
Happily Ever After

The Chinese capture the essence of life in their folktale of a vase who lamented it was cracked and thus leaked half of its water being carried back from the river. Yet, the wise owner planted seeds along that side of the road, and a row of flowers grew there. Meaning that while the other vase brought back more water, the cracked vase nourished beauty, but only because the girl was wise enough to come up with a brilliant solution. How many times have you complained and destroyed things because you did not see the beauty and potential of your metaphorically cracked vases?

"New information is always grounds for a new decision."
– Barbara Wotherspoon

Sometimes perfect looks different than you expect, so you don't see it as perfect. Upset, you usually don't think straight. Marriage brings out aspects of a person that are intolerable. Expectations change after marrying. Behavior that had been okay as a girlfriend isn't okay as a wife. What you do now reflects on your husband, so it annoys him when you look silly, stupid, unconventional, weird, or different. Dating he thought your mistakes cute or was too polite to point them out. The wedding band changed everything.

> *To the degree you are struggling whether to divorce or not is to the degree you are not being true to yourself.*

When you employ the motto, "You don't have to succeed, but you do have to try," you discover that you are smarter than you realized. You master things that previously intimidated you. Not fearing failure, you try everything of interest, like sampling the smorgasbord called life. The goal is not to become a master at that task, but merely to attempt it. Think experiment. You succeed by trying. You lose in life when lacking the courage to go to places you'd like to go and do the things you'd like to do.

I went as far as Tibet, Bali and Siberia to seek answers.

The deliberation whether to stay in your marriage or end it can be short and easy, or drawn out and painful. It depends on your willingness to give up the illusions of what you think a marriage should be. It depends on your willingness to give up being right and proving your husband wrong. It depends on your willingness to give up shame, blame, guilt, anger, apathy, and pride.

Dating in China was hard because there were few foreigners. The Chinese men didn't appeal because they didn't arouse me sexually, perhaps because they lacked tension. I dated a Texan who I'd met online and inspired to come teach in China. He broke it off after a few months, but we remained friends. However, when he dumped me as a friend, I thought, "I need a different kind of man."

In a tangle of hair he found me,
Setting fire to my own hair.
In a tangle of hair he left me,
Knowing he couldn't be happy there.
Spinning up to the sun, and inside out,
It was time for a new kind of man,
One who'd calm away my doubts,
And stop me before I ran.

A Canadian high school principal asked me out. He ran a Nova Scotia program for Chinese students planning to go abroad to English-speaking universities. However, our romance only happened because I listened to the quiet voice.

Quiet Voice: "Interview at his school."
Me: "But I love my job, I don't want to move."
Quiet Voice: "Go."

He interviewed me for two hours, and the rest is history. Our marriage works because he is a kind and patient man. Raising my level of consciousness to joy allowed me to see that arrogance was not sexy. My husband loves to travel almost as much I do. Together we visited Hong Kong, Macau, Japan, South Korea, got engaged in Taiwan, Cambodia, Laos, Singapore, Malaysia, Thailand, Vietnam, Bali, Baja California, and taken the Trans-Siberian train from Beijing to Moscow going through Mongolia, a five-day escapade that included being left behind at a train station. I turned sixty somewhere in Siberia. We look forward to golfing in every state in America and every province in Canada. And the sex? He makes me come by just kissing me.

> *You know safety is a funny thing,*
> *it does not have a sexy ring,*
> *but safe is sane and cures what's wrong*
> *and makes forever a happy song.*

The level of consciousness of most people is at anger and pride. Thus, newscasters report on the most horrible tragedies, as that's what resonates with the most people. But what if pain and misery are markers in the road? What if they are literal stop signs warning you to slow down, to take a different path and detour around that rotten road? Joy lays hidden inside every person, virtually dormant, beneath layers of petrified muck, generations old, so deeply buried that many people wallow in depression, shrink in fear, explode in anger, ruminate in guilt, and reminisce in grief.

Joy is a simple emotion. It has neither obligation nor agenda. It has neither loyalty nor demand. It expects nothing and is everything. It gives and receives in a continuous loop like the infinity symbol. It needs no one and yet includes everyone. It needs no affirmation, no praise, nor any notice. If criticized, it is not diminished. No one can give you joy. No one can take away your joy. It requires neither health, nor wealth, nor education. It does require a mind, body, and soul. It is the epitome of self-confidence.

Marriages are hard for most everyone. Even good marriages have to work at keeping theirs good. This book was written so that you don't have to waste so much time doing things by trial and error, so that you can learn new ways to restore calm, and ultimately bring peace and harmony to your family. Think of this book as your new best friend when you're down and need a helping hand.

You know you are resisting whenever you are sad or mad. God wants you to be happy. He wants you to shine as the wonderful creature you are, to spread love and joy. You started this journey with questions and overwhelm. You got clarity and understanding from doing the exercises in each chapter. You forged a new you. Each exercise expanded your awareness and made you malleable enough to change. You expended a lot of effort to reinvent yourself. You sloughed so many skins that your emotional character changed. Clarity morphed you into a strong, confident woman.

> *"At the center of your being you have the answer;*
> *you know who you are and you know what you want."*
> **– Lao Tzu**

This metamorphosis purged the destructive emotions of shame, grief, guilt, apathy, desire, fear, anger, and pride. By emancipating yourself from these sabotaging behaviors, you elevate yourself into higher levels of consciousness. Learning to calm allows you to hear your quiet voice. Listening to your quiet voice is like God answering when you call. To learn that this quiet voice was within you and available at all times was to confirm that you are not alone.

To know that you have a direct line to God is so empowering that confidence swells into courage. Courage makes you bold enough to surrender your ego and try new ways to deal with your husband or your ex. By learning to remain neutral you no longer felt compelled to defend yourself. By not defending yourself, you no longer trigger your husband to defend himself. This new ability enables you to defuse upsets, your own and conflicts with him. Your willingness to give up fear, anger, and pride further improve your communication skills to where you discuss issues rather than fight.

Your accepting your husband, without any agenda to change him, means you respect him as an equal and put you both on the same team. You both want harmony. Reason can be a helpmate instead of a weapon. Redefining winning to mean you both have to win shifts you from being enemies to cooperating as teammates and allows unconditional love to sprout out of the manure accumulated in your marriage which came from fear, anger, and pride. Your grace enables you to surrender your need to be right, your need to make him wrong, and to see that good and bad does not exist, and that differences are merely interesting, not bones of contention. Your ability to float up to the clouds gives you God's perspective that the world is just as it needs to be, evolving at its designed pace, and that it's not your job to change or doubt God.

You bought this book because you wanted to change your life. You tried out the exercises like trying on new clothes to see which fit best and which most suited you. You cleaned out your closet of shabby thoughts and the ones that no longer fit. You donated those to the universe. Having thoughts that are light and comfortable make you smile and feel good about yourself. Your thoughts reflect the new you, authentically representing the woman you cleaved by diligently learning all the skills you needed to tailor-fit your body, mind and soul.

You are a hero in your own eyes. You achieved what you feared impossible because you didn't give up, because you persevered through the quicksand of old habits and broke out of the chrysalis of pain. You shed skins that grew too tight and puffed up big with the expectation of better times in your future. You proved that anything is possible, and that the impossible just takes longer.

> *"Why waste time being sad when*
> *you can waste time being happy?"*
> – **Melissa Harris**, age six

Recommended Reading

Read in Any Order:

- Alda, Alan, *If I Understood You, Would I Have This Look on My Face? My Adventures in the Art and Science of Relating and Communicating*
- Biskind, Sandra, *Codebreaker: Discover the Password to Unlocking the Best Version of You*
- Blanchard, Ken, *The One Minute Manager*
- Brown, Brené, *The Gifts of Imperfection: Let Go of Who You Think You're Supposed to Be and Embrace Who You Are*
- Brown, Brené, *Dare to Lead: Brave work. Tough conversations. Whole Hearts.*
- Brown, Brené, *Daring Greatly and Rising Strong at Work*
- Brown, Stuart, Play: *How It Shapes the Brain, Opens the Imagination, and Invigorates the Soul*

- Canfield, Jack, *The Success Principles: How to Get from Where You Are to Where You Want to Be*
- Carnegie, Dale, *How to Win Friends & Influence People*
- Chapman, Gary, *The 5 Love Languages, The Secret to Love That Lasts*
- Coyle, Daniel, *The Culture Code: The Secrets of Highly Successful Groups*
- Dunn, Elizabeth, *Happy Money, The Science of Happier Spending*
- Dyer, Wayne, *Erroneous Zones*
- Estes, Clarissa, *Women Who Run With the Wolves: Myths and Stories of the Wild Woman Archetype*
- Gladwell, Malcolm, *The Tipping Point: How Little Things Can Make a Big Difference*
- Gladwell, Malcolm, *Blink: The Power of Thinking Without Thinking*
- Gottman, John, *The Seven Principles for Making Marriage Work*
- Greenberger, Dennis, *Mind Over Mood*
- Hawkins, David, *Power vs. Force*
- Hawkins, David, *Along the Path to Enlightenment: 365 Daily Reflections*
- Hawkins, David, *Dealing with the Crazy Makers in Your Life: Setting Boundaries on Unhealthy Relationships*
- Hawkins, David, *When Loving Him is Hurting You: Hope and Help for Women Dealing with Narcissism and Emotional Abuse*
- Hawkins, David, *When Pleasing Others is Hurting You: Finding God's Patterns for Healthy Relationships*
- Hay, Louise, *You Can Heal Your Life*
- Johnson, Spencer, *Who Moved My Cheese?*
- Kahneman, Daniel, *Thinking: Fast and Slow*
- Katie, Byron, *Loving What Is, Four Questions That Can Change Your Life*

- Katie, Byron, *I Need Your Love—Is That True?*
- Keller, Gary, *The One Thing: The Surprisingly Simple Truth Behind Extraordinary Results*
- Lakein, Alan, *How to Get Control of Your Time and Your Life*
- Licht, Aliza, *Leave Your Mark, Land Your Dream Job. Kill It in Your Career. Rock Social Media.*
- Mandino, Og, *The Greatest Salesman in the World*
- Mandino, Og, *The Greatest Salesman in the World, Part II, The End of the Story*
- Shinn, Florence, *The Game of Life*
- Welch, Edward, *When People Are Big and God is Small: Overcoming Peer Pressure, Codependency and the Fear of Man*

Other Books by Kathryn MacIntyre

(formerly Kathryn Velikanje)

Everyday Circus

Zebras Paint Themselves Rainbow (Silly Willy's World) (Volume 1)

A Bike of Bees (Silly Willy's World) (Volume 2)

A is for ALLIGATOR (Silly Willy's ALPHABET) (Volume 1)

A is for ALLIGATOR (Chinese) (Silly Willy's Alphabet) (Volume 1)
(Chinese Edition)

B is for BOYS and BEES (Silly Willy's ALPHABET) (Volume 2)

C is for CRAZY CATS (Silly Willy's ALPHABET) (Volume 3)

D is for DRAGON (Silly Willy's ALPHABET) (Volume 4)

E is for ELEPHANT (Silly Willy's ALPHABET) (Volume 5)

E is for ELEPHANT (Chinese) (Silly Willy's Alphabet) (Volume 5)
(Chinese Edition)

F is for FACE (Silly Willy's ALPHABET) (Volume 6)

G is for GIRLY GIRLS (Silly Willy's ALPHABET) (Volume 7)

H is for HORSE (Silly Willy's ALPHABET) (Volume 8)

I is for ICE CREAM (Silly Willy's ALPHABET) (Volume 9)

Acknowledgments

My biggest thanks go to my daughters, Melissa and Anna, who are my mentors and closest friends. To their dad for making me a mom, the greatest joy I have ever known. To my Rolfers Patricia Wandler, Daniel Frank, Rich Goodstein, Gary Gilbert, and Saviera Claudia Studen without whom I wouldn't and couldn't have melted my armor. To Richard Steinberg who made all of our lives better. To Don Duncan for letting me go without a fight. To Pam Oslie for envisioning, encouraging, befriending, and believing in me. To Steve Martin who invited me into his home and asked me back. To all my Rolfing clients for giving me some of the best years of my life. To my colleagues in China, we bonded as a family of ex-pats, and forged lifetime kinship. To my Chinese students, thank you for letting me be a mom and mentor, and for taking all the love I had to give.

Huge thanks and gratitude to my husband, Bernie, who has the patience and wisdom to press his lips when angry and stay silent. Heartfelt gratitude to Sine and Mary-Jo, who are always there when I'm upset, yet who always believe I will bounce back even better. To Darryl who made those first months living in Nova Scotia much more fun. To

Kara, Curtis, Brenda, Hughie, and the entire MacIntyre, MacMullin, and MacDonald clans who have made me feel like I belong. To my brother who I admire and cherish. To my Aunt Pat who loves me like a daughter and who demonstrated that it's okay for women to go to college, travel the world, be independent, and most of all is my biggest fan. To those passed over, namely my mom and Grandma Niver, who daily cheer me on and give wise counsel. To Sandra Biskind for showing me what love is, who is so compassionate that just gazing into her eyes brings healing. To Jack Canfield for beaming with godlike benevolence while I floundered scared and angry. To Patty Aubrey who believed in me and encouraged to go out alone and teach my stuff, rather than shadow Jack Canfield.

To my dad who believed I could and would succeed and was proud when I did. To Shaundi Kuper-Sweddal who stayed for five days in our home, and always makes me feel special and adored. To Barbara Wotherspoon who has been a mentor, a coach, a friend, and mothered me for years. To Jessica Duncan who has worked hard for us to remain close friends. To my cousin Julie who I've always admired, who makes me feel like a rock star, and who always makes me laugh. To Emily Benson for coaching me when I panicked over leaving China. To Elizabeth Beringer for taking me under her wing to learn Feldenkrais. To Debb Hanks who was the highlight of the Canfield retreat, who was my accountability partner and best friend thereafter. To Pongsri and Robert Dempsey who traveled all the way to China to test the viability of a business together. To Alisia Leavitt for editing my book about joy and culling out what I didn't know I knew. To Angela Lauria for developing The Author Incubator which brought forth this book, a compilation of a lifetime of wisdom gleaned from around the world. Thank you to David Hancock and the Morgan James Publishing team for helping me bring this book to print.

Thank You

Thanks so much for reading my book. I hope it brought moments of peace and harmony to your life and marriage. I hope you have clarity and understanding in new ways.

Life and marriage isn't always easy or fun. I hope you found that some of these tools brought ease and calm and diffused some of your upsets. If you've achieved all you needed or wanted, congratulations! However, if you feel you'd like personal guiding and would like to work more in-depth, please email me at KathrynMacIntyreJOY@gmail.com.

About the Author

 Kathryn MacIntyre is a life coach who teaches successful, professional women on how to make their marriages happy. Or, if divorce is the best option, how to build a new and better life. She has lived in five countries and has gone as far as Tibet and Siberia to seek how to thrive in marriage.

After two divorces, she had epiphanies that would have solved the problems of her past marriages, but those solutions were seven to twenty years too late. Thus, she found ways to get epiphanies to solve current problems, and is now happily married. After teaching thousands of people around the world, she became a life coach.

As a certified Rolfer, Kathryn had a hands-on knowledge of how pain hardens muscles and causes headaches, migraines, and limited flexibility. Being a certified laughter yoga instructor, she teaches clients how to use laughter to elevate from low energy levels such as shame, guilt, fear, depression, overwhelm, and anger to higher levels such as courage, willingness and acceptance. Studying Feldenkrais, she learned how to teach self-awareness so that people can fix themselves.

A graduate from the University of California at Santa Barbara, Kathryn is an avid traveler, reader, cyclist, paddleboard enthusiast, and golfer. She is the author of twelve children's picture books, co-authored seventeen children's songs, and volunteers at the YMCA Immigrant Centre. She splits her time between living with her husband in Nova Scotia, Canada, and visiting family in San Diego, California.

Endnotes

1   https://www.wf-lawyers.com/divorce-statistics-and-facts/
2   https://www.encyclopedia.com/people/philosophy-and-religion/philosophy-biographies/lao-tzu%3E
3   Ibid
4   http://www.who.int/mediacentre/factsheets/fs369/en/
5   https://www.huffpost.com/entry/happiness-tips_b_1739238
6   https://www.chakras.info/solar-plexus-chakra/
7   https://health.usnews.com/wellness/articles/the-benefits-of-using-a-standing-desk
8   https://www.mindfulfitness.com/
9   http://usatoday30.usatoday.com/news/health/2006-05-25-backward-running_x.html

CPSIA information can be obtained
at www.ICGtesting.com
Printed in the USA
JSHW031901140121
10859JS00009B/22

9 781631 951046